Nail Your College Essay

Stick Your Opening Line
Hone Your Narrative Voice
Capture Your Personal Story

Jan Rooker

Published by Rooker Associates LLC
58 Pine Street
New Canaan, CT 06840
www.janrooker.com

Published by: Rooker Associates, LLC, 58 Pine Street, New
Canaan, CT 06840

Important Notes: Readers should be aware that Internet
Web sites given as sources for further information may have
changed or disappeared between the time this was
published and the time when it is read.

While the publisher/author has used all best efforts in preparing
this book, she makes no representations or warranties with
respect to the accuracy or completeness of the contents of this
book and specifically disclaims any implied warranties of
merchantability or fitness for a particular purpose. No warranty
may be created or extended by sales representatives or written
sales materials. The advice and strategies presented herein may
not be suitable for your situation. Please consult with a
professional where appropriate. The publisher and author shall
not be liable for any loss or damages alleged to be caused,
directly or indirectly by the information or links contained in
this document.

ISBN 978-0-615-30319-2

Permissions:
All of the more than 32 student writers whose essays were used wholly or in part have given their permission for use of their written words in this book.

Admissions officers from the three universities—University of Virginia, Tufts University, and Oregon State University—whose words were quoted from their web sites have given their permission to quote the words.

Cover Design:
The cover was designed by Nellys Li.

*This book is dedicated to
all the students past and present who have shared
their dreams and ideas and writing
and who have helped me remember, even when I
sometimes forgot, that Huck Finn lives.*

*And in memory, with gratitude, joy and love,
to BKC who, on any given day,
would drop everything and get me to
go fishing with him.*

Contents

Introduction

Colleges Have a Mission

When a college admissions committee evaluates you for admission to a class, it is guided by this question: Will you succeed and contribute to our college community and our society? Factors bearing on this question might include intellectual curiosity and promise, motivation, over-all energy, leadership skills, integrity, judgment, self-image, non-traditional learning ability, realistic self-assessment, independence, originality, preparation, special skills and talents, resilience, etc. No student will have all of these qualities, but most students will have some.

Of course, some of these factors will be obvious to the admissions committee from your academic record or from test results, while others will be apparent through teacher and guidance counselor recommendations. Further traits will emerge during interviews—if there are any, or through additional submissions, such as an art or writing portfolio, an athletic tape, or a talent audition, if appropriate. However, for almost all students, the unique qualities you possess will shine through in your personal essay. Since the essay is the only place where you—the student—make these qualities known to an admissions committee, the essay offers a great opportunity to stand out from every other applicant.

My Mission

My main goal is to help you recognize the personal qualities and characteristics you have, to help you value and support them, and to assist you in bringing them forward so they will be evident in your essay.

Further I want to help you recognize and use your "authentic" voice. This voice is the one you use when you talk to good friends discussing the things you care about most. It is also the voice you may use when you talk to yourself. I suspect, though, that this voice is not the one that most of you use in school essays. You may even consider your authentic voice to be too informal for writing an essay, especially one which could determine which college you will attend. I want you to know, however, that this voice is not too informal. It is genuine. It is, therefore, the voice you want. It is my hope that I will convince you to nurture this voice and use it to tell a story. This story will be a story that only you can tell because it is, after all, a story about you. Your story, in your own words, and in your most genuine voice, offers the basis for an effective personal admissions essay.

Ultimately I want you to recognize that an effective essay will distinguish you from other students and will forge a connection with a college admissions counselor, a connection that will make you memorable.

My Background

I have been a college consultant for almost 15 years. Prior to this I taught high school English in Ridgewood, NJ. Each year I visit numerous colleges across the country. I graduated from Cornell University (BA), Stanford University (MA), and Columbia University (MA). My Web site is: www.janrooker.com. My Email is: jan@janrooker.com

Chapter 1

WHAT COLLEGES ARE LOOKING FOR—WHEN THEY ASK YOU TO WRITE A PERSONAL ESSAY

When colleges ask you to write your application essay they want to know you better. They want to know about the person behind the numbers on your transcript and on your SAT score report. But they want to know more. They want to know what has happened to you, and, maybe, what has happened in your family. They want to know how you see yourself and what you think and talk about, the kind of stories you tell. What moves you? What do you dream about? How do you react to a challenge, and what is your tolerance for risk? How do you differ from others who are your same age? How are you different from others who want to be on the same campus? How do you see yourself developing as you go forward into the future?

In Their Own Words, What Do Colleges Say?

Some colleges explain in detail to students what they are looking for in an essay. Tufts University, for example, gives students clear insights into what they think makes an essay distinctive and engaging. At the admissions portion of the school's Web site (www.admissions.tufts.edu), you will find a number of successful essays that worked for the admissions counselors—look under the heading "Discovering Voice: Essays That Matter" In describing these essays, the Office of Admissions says:

> These pieces captured the distinct voices of these young men and women, and forged a powerful and affective human connection with their readers. They truly helped to set these students apart in our applicant pool. They

13

compelled, magnetized, and fascinated us. They demonstrated creativity and illuminated curiosity.

Here's an excerpt from one of the essays. Olga, the student who wrote it, was admitted to the Tufts University, Class of 2010.

> I wear whatever I want to wear, not the in-one-second-and-out-the-next-I-paid-enough-money- for-this-to-feed-a-small-underdeveloped-nation clothing that everyone around me seems to wear, and I've actually had someone approach me just to say, "Look, I'm wearing an Olga hat," when I barely knew her name.
>
> I don't throw things away, and I can still remember the phone number of my second grade best friend that I haven't actually spoken to in seven years. I wear kids' sweatshirts and many of my poems are about the loss of innocence, though they don't usually start out that way.

You can imagine what the admissions staff was thinking when they read this opening to the essay. "Wow! Who is this kid? I want to know more!" Your essay can spark the same excitement—if it is authentic.

Some colleges actually go further in that they help you to understand what your high school English teacher always tried to get you to understand, the difference between telling and showing. On the University of Virginia undergraduate admissions Web site, Senior Assistant Dean of Admission Parke Muth says:

> A good essay is not good because of the topic but because of the voice. A good writer can make any topic interesting, and a weak writer can make even the most dramatic topic a bore. Students need only to recall the difference between two simple concepts—showing and telling. A good essay always shows; a weak essay always tells.

What Colleges Are Looking For

Check the University of Virginia Web site (www.virginia.edu/undergradadmission/writingtheessay) to see the rest of Parke Muth's advice about essays.

What Colleges Don't Want from Your Personal Essay

Colleges have your transcripts and test scores. They don't want—or need—an essay that lists your academic accomplishments in narrative form. Nor do they want a thesis-based five paragraph essay in which you prove—using an introduction, three body paragraphs, and a conclusion—that "Competing in tennis matches is an important activity in my life. It has taught me perseverance, discipline and how to overcome a setback." When one student I worked with, Katie, realized this, she said, "It's too bad, but I guess they are not looking for the standard essay we've been taught our whole lives to write so well." She couldn't have been more right!

Colleges also do not want a well-researched expository paper on why a historic figure is worth being revered or why a current crisis is so important nationally. I can understand why you might think that they do, as several of the essay questions on the Common Application (www.commonapp.org) may lead you to this conclusion. But an expository essay, even on these topics, is not the kind of essay that colleges hope to read. Colleges are also not looking for an essay that speaks to an unasked admissions question that you are sure you have guessed the answer to and which you think you can explain just the way the college wants you to. In fact, the worst thing you can do is to write an essay answering a question in a way that you suppose the admissions office will think is "right."

A story which illustrates the results of the practice of trying to guess what an admissions office wants to hear is told on the University of Virginia's Web site. When the university asked applicants to write an essay about an invention or creation from the past that was important to them, over 1,000 applicants in one year wrote about the Declaration of Independence. Applicants assumed that because the University of Virginia was founded by Thomas Jefferson who authored the Declaration, this would be a good answer. The college points out, however, that because so many of the submitted essays were so similar, the admissions officers were unable to distinguish between the applicants. So the last thing you want to do is submit an essay in which you answer the question as you think the college wants it answered. You may be thinking that if essays such as these are coherent and grammatically correct, then they must be good essays. And although they may be, they will not distinguish you; and, thus, they cannot make you memorable.

Distinguishing yourself and being memorable are important objectives. These objectives were also stressed recently during a question-and-answer session I attended with Stanford University's Assistant Dean of Undergraduate Admissions, DeAngela Burns-Wallace. The question one consultant posed was: what is Stanford looking for in its "supplemental" admission's question that asks, "Virtually all of Stanford's undergraduates live on campus. What would you want your freshman year roommate to know about you? Tell us something about you that will help your roommate—and us—know you better." The question one consultant asked was, "What kinds of things are you looking for and what has worked as an interesting answer in the past for this question?" Ms. Burns excused herself from answering this. She said if she did answer, Stanford would get 300 essays on that exact topic next year. How would this help them distinguish between applicants?

What Colleges Are Looking For

So, Then, What Should Guide Your Essay?

Be your self—as well as you can. Set out to know yourself and then share that true self with the admission counselor who will read your file.

In Chapter 2, I believe that you will come to understand what having your own authentic voice means. In Chapter 3, I believe you will see how to know who you are, what your story will be, and that your story will distinguish you. In Chapter 4, you will read some examples of effective personal application essays. First, though, let us briefly look at one short sample so we better understand the specific goal toward which we are heading.

Essay Sample

The following excerpt (Version 1) is the beginning of an essay with an authentic voice. Version 2 is the beginning of the same student's essay as it was revised by the student and her well-meaning English tutor. Read and compare them.

Version 1: Bart

"Well, at least somebody jumped the jump," was the first thing I heard when I looked up from the ground on the far side of the jump and saw my friend, Marge.

We were at the Vermont Summer Festival and I was participating in my first real horse show— riding Bart, that is. I had been jumping a 3'3" oxer. The jump was situated uphill, and you need a lot of pace to jump uphill. I had asked Bart to jump without enough pace and he had stopped short—unfortunately, I didn't. I had catapulted over the jump.

My friend Marge who was watching from the sidelines laughingly said, "Well, at least, someone jumped the jump." She was being funny, and in a way saying, "It's okay that you fell off." Anyway, because my feet had hit the ground I was out of that class. But because I would be able to participate in another class, I got right up and right back on. That's how it is with me.

Version 2: <u>Riding Is My Favorite Activity</u>

I began riding when my mom gave me riding lessons for my sixth birthday. The riding ring is where you can find me on most Saturdays and Sundays, and every day after school. Becoming a horse back rider has helped me to learn many life lessons: perseverance, discipline and how to overcome set-backs.

(What followed were paragraphs two, three and four, each respectively, about perseverance, discipline and overcoming setbacks. The conclusion repeated the ideas of the first paragraph.)

Which of these essays do you find most interesting, most lively, and most informative regarding the student who wrote them? Both essays reveal that the student is an accomplished equestrian but the first excerpt "shows" it, while the second essay "tells" it. The first one also shows through its voice that the writer is determined, spunky, humorous, not easily embarrassed and strong enough to challenge the will of her equally strong-minded horse, Bart. The second, well, it shows she's learned to write a "standard" formulaic essay. Put yourself in the role of an admissions officer. Will you be wowed by the authentic person? Or will you be wowed by the person who sounds like a five-paragraph student robot? Whom would you most want to admit?

Recognizing the Personal Essay

Somewhere along the line, as you write your applications for admissions to college, colleges will also ask you to write about why you want to study on their campus and what it is you think you want to study. What do you aspire to do in life? How will you interact on campus? Based on your current inclinations, what will you choose to support and involve yourself in when you get on campus? What do you see as your role in the future? When colleges ask these questions and others like them, they will usually be asking them in some kind of supplemental essay, like Stanford's question about the roommate. This is not usually the stuff of a personal essay. So this is not what we are talking about here. What we are talking about here, in this book, is the main personal essay, and the instructions often offered for this essay are just, "Write an essay on a topic of your choice."

Chapter 2

YOUR AUTHENTIC VOICE

What Does "Being Authentic" Mean?

The "best" college essays not only let a reader in—to get to know the person who is the writer— they also have open, honest, and truthful voices— authentic voices.

Fred Hargadon, past Dean of Admissions at Princeton and Stanford Universities, and Swarthmore College, has often been a featured speaker at the annual Harvard Summer Institute on College Admissions. He's so talented, in fact, that a few years ago, Fred was the welcome speaker, the key-note speaker, the farewell speaker and a conference session speaker. He believes that storytelling is a powerful way to communicate with others. A story with its specific details, told in the uniquely authentic voice of the teller, communicates who the person is. Fred also recommends storytelling to students writing their college admissions essays.

That storytelling is an excellent approach to communicating seems clear. Stories can impart information better than most other forms of communication. They are better than lists, better than outlines, and better than persuasive arguments. Additionally stories engage us more deeply, create connections more quickly, and prove themselves memorable more often.

Throughout the conference, Fred demonstrated his storytelling approach. At one point he told the following story and I've done my best to recall exactly what he said. One day during the application reading period in January or February, he had been reading a number of college essays from prospective freshmen. Tired of reading essays lacking personality and voice, he came out of his office saying, "Where are all the real Huck Finns?"

I understood this reference immediately; I had admired the spirited spontaneity and open voice of Huck Finn for a long time. Samuel Clemens' Huck is an unselfconscious, candid story-teller. He tells you what he has seen and heard without editing out things he thinks might offend you and without being afraid to let you see who he is. He does not tell a story he thinks will please you, but one he feels is important to get out there. And for the most part he seems to like himself, even when he finds himself deviating from the opinions and practices of the majority of others in his community. Unlike Huck, some students have lost their original, authentic voices. For fear of offending, or for fear of being embarrassed by an unkind teacher or judgmental peers, they have hidden their genuine voices.

In *The Adventures of Huckleberry Finn,* we find Huck allowing himself to be civilized by the Widow Douglas and her maiden sister, Miss Watson. He agrees to this, even though he feels many of society's practices are silly, only because Tom Sawyer tells Huck that he is forming a gang, and in order to be in it, Huck has to live with the widow and be respectable. Huck, making no apologies for his view of society, tells us that one evening after supper, the widow:

> …got out her book and learned me about Moses and the bulrushes, and I was in a sweat to find out all about him; but by and by she let it out that Moses had been dead a considerable long time; so then I didn't care no more about him; because I don't take no stock in dead people.

Huck goes on:

> Pretty soon I wanted to smoke, and asked the widow to let me. But she wouldn't. She said it was a mean practice and wasn't clean, and I must try to not do it anymore. That is just the way with some people. They get down on a thing when they don't know nothing

about it. Here she was a-bothering about Moses, which was no kin to her, and no use to anybody, being gone, you see, yet finding a power of fault with me for doing a thing that had some good in it. And she took snuff too; of course that was all right, because she done it herself.

I guess you could say that Huck is an individual who says and does what he feels is right. He isn't afraid to let you know what he thinks about things, even if he has to tell you that he is confused, or unsure. Because of his honesty, his *authenticity,* and his story telling ability, we like Huck. I do and you probably will, too, if you reread his story.

But even if you don't, I hope that by the time you finish reading all, or some, of the essays in this book, you will be able to say with me, in answer to Fred Hargadon, "Huck Finn still lives!" He can still be heard—in the voices and souls of our youth.

An Authentic Voice Knows Itself

An authentic voice speaks with candor—some might call this abandon—and doesn't second-guess itself, and is not self-conscious.

The first student I ever guided in writing his college essay was Mark, an attendee of a boys' Catholic high school. His essays for school had always been written in a formal, scholarly style, in an anonymous voice. He was accustomed to censoring any personal voice out of his papers for fear of offending the priests who taught his classes and whom Mark had been taught to treat formally. He had little idea of what his real voice was or that he could allow it to come forth in an essay—especially his essay for college admission.

One day as we were leaving the library where we had been working on SAT materials, Mark spotted a handicapped acquaintance who had been learning to bowl with Mark's help for many of the previous weeks. While this work was part of Mark's community service at school, it was clearly more. The handicapped fellow was way across the parking lot of the library, but Mark yelled loudly, waving his arms to attract his friend's attention.

"Hey, Larry—how are you, buddy?" yelled Mark.

"Mark, I'm so glad to see you!" Larry yelled back.

"You know you really like other people and would never miss a chance to say hello," I said. "And they love you back. Look how glad Larry is that you greeted him."

A version of this became the first line of Mark's essay. It read, unabashedly: "I love people, and people love me."

The essay went on to tell about Mark's dedication to the community service he did after school, as well as about his summer job in a baseball facility where, in the batting cage, he had had the opportunity to coach a struggling young eight-year-old, who had been afraid of the batting machine. This boy became a successful hitter under Mark's friendly tutelage.

The best part of this story about writing Mark's college admissions essay, though, is that after the essay was written, Mark, several times in one evening, took his essay into the kitchen where his mother was cooking and said, "Mom, listen to this essay. It is so me!" Mark knew that he had found his voice and he was proud.

The authentic voice, then, is your true voice. It has power. It is the real you thinking to yourself and sharing your thoughts. To use this voice effectively it is important to find out who you are, to learn to recognize yourself and to make distinctions between yourself and others. Find something you like about yourself—or that others like about you—and tell that story in the most positive terms you can, just as Mark learned to do.

Authentic Student Voices

I believe you will hear the confidence and the sense of knowing in the following excerpts from essays written by students:

- I play trombone with the high school Jazz II Band. There is a Jazz I Band but, truthfully Jazz II rocks harder than they do. During a song we are allowed to take certain liberties with the melody and rhythms, after we finish rehearsing either the director says, "Good job," or "Don't do that again." I would like to tell you the former happens more than the latter, but I am about 50-50.

- My best friend Alex has been my best friend since second grade. I don't know whether our friendship was cemented the summer we tried to build the soapbox, or whether it was cemented every day we spent after middle school at the bus stop when we talked for 45 minutes sitting on the curbside, or whether it's been our recent discussions about atheism, god, politics, and life.

- I can't say that I've been scarred. However, in every elementary school class picture, I had to stand in the back row. I never got to hold the black and white sign with the grade and teacher's name like the cute little kids in the front row did. Worst of all, by third grade, I was past children's shoe size 5, so I could not fit into those cool light-up gym sneakers. I never understood why my friends would tell me, "I wish I could be as tall as you." I mean, why would someone want to be as tall as I am?

- A famous track coach once said, "Hurdlers are sprinters with a problem." He was right. The problem is that I'm not satisfied with simply *running* down the track. It just seems so mundane! ....When I first joined my high school's track team I knew right away that I wanted to be a hurdler. The challenge of having to leap over one bar after another and still keep on sprinting seemed so exciting. And to make things a little spicier, in every race there is always the element of danger. You or one of the guys you're racing could trip over his hurdle and take a dive towards the track, and create a human train wreck. I like to think of hurdling as the NASCAR of Track & Field; it gets more spectators than the other events because people want to see some carnage.

- I have been blessed with creativity and passion for learning that is uncommon in my peers. Unfortunately, I have also been hindered by multiple issues: a 40 percent hearing deficit and an auditory processing disorder. While the late diagnosis of these problems has affected my academic transcript negatively, their eventual discovery has led to a new and improved me.

- The reach, the steals, the passes, the shots, the fouls, the ejections, the pushing, and shoving are all factors involved when playing water polo. The sport is grueling and aggressive, but that is why I am addicted.

- Teaching Sunday school surprises me—I find it is enjoyable to hang out with a bunch of 7th and 8th graders, even though they constantly want my attention and demand to be around me...and over time I have come to admire their carefree spirits because, unlike me, they don't take life so seriously.

- I pull the heavy glass door open and enter the studio. With a wide smile, I greet the nine fresh faces who are dressed in their pink shirts, black jazz pants, and black tap shoes. I sit down to lace up my own black leather tap shoes. The Head of the School gives me a quick hug as another year of teaching dance begins. Then she introduces me to the nine five and six year olds. Today I am Miss Karina...

26

- When 20 four-year-olds come screaming into the room you better make sure there is something to do. Setting up for arts and crafts at the Nature Center was my job, and I learned right away that finger paints were out of the question. Markers were a big enough hassle—with kids writing on the tables, walls and pretty much anywhere possible. Three seconds after I finished putting out the supplies, all of the kids came running down the stairs and into the room. Art began.

- I don't want a job in a cubicle; I want a job where I can wear a backwards baseball cap to work. Don't get me wrong, though, I can wear a blazer and tie with the best of them. However, I don't want a job where attire comes before doing something I love, in a comfortable atmosphere, where fun and humor is expected. I feel I have many talents. Yet, even writing this essay is too confining for me.

- With that, the bell rang to end my first physics class. Students to my left and right scurried to fit their belongings in their backpacks and escape Honors Physics. I, on the other hand, sat there in awe, trying to absorb what I had just heard. Without leaving my seat, I immediately opened my physics textbook to chapter one to see if physics was just as difficult and exciting as Mr. Hastava made it seem. Within seconds I was enticed by the fascinating definitions and magnificent mathematical expressions that were written across the page. I had never seen anything so complex, yet, so beautifully simple. Before I knew it the bell for the start of second period had already rung. I quickly stuffed my textbook into my backpack and sprinted to my next class.

- If someone told me I was going to write my college essay about being a hot-glue gun queen, I would have said they were crazy. But the truth is hot-gluing has

- turned me into a crafty-social butterfly. Not only do I use my glue gun for an easy fix to repair things around my house, I also use it to create colorful and bold cards and special cakes for social events. My friends and family have begun to insist on them for every holiday. Hot-gluing allows me to quickly and easily explode my creativity into my projects.

- Before I had even finished tying the first knot, Ryan was standing up, demanding that the rope be passed around. There was no doubt in my mind that he did not actually want to practice tying anything but rather distract himself by maliciously flicking his eleven year old friends. I was the newly appointed Senior Patrol Leader, standing in front of 20 out-of-control young Boy Scouts, who by the end of their day could not have sat still to save their own lives. They were punching each other's shoulders, kicking each other's legs, and asking questions relevant to something only in their imaginations. It was great to be in charge.

The students in the above excerpts have begun to have a feeling of who they are. More importantly, they have begun to like the people they are, and to look forward to sharing this new found personal side of themselves with others.

When the college search and application process leads to discovering who you are, it goes beyond the process and develops into a really rewarding experience. Then the experience becomes positive, a growth experience, and often delivers a genuine "aha!" moment. When it unfolds this way, it is thrilling.

Trusting Others to Appreciate Your Authentic Voice

So let's assume you are ready to begin and that you clearly know your own voice. Yet, here you may still encounter a common problem. It isn't always easy to relax, to feel comfortable enough to talk in a genuine voice. Yet, your essay should sound like a story you enjoy telling to someone with whom you feel comfortable.

To help yourself relax you have to forget about the college official or the room full of admissions officers who will read your essay. Instead you should imagine talking to someone whom you trust—your best friend's older sister, whom you like, but also look up to. Another person you might want to imagine talking to is the aunt who adores you and always brings you little presents or the uncle who takes you to ball games. Sometimes I tell my students to think about their fairy godmothers—a fairy godmother loves you, pulls for you, and would do anything to help you. Tell your story to her.

Martha Graham, Marianne Williamson, and Nelson Mandela have some thoughts that shed light on the courage it takes to allow yourself to be, in public, the "you" that you are. Revealing the authentic you to others is not something that is easy for anyone, even important, well-known people. Martha Graham, a famous dancer and choreographer, said:

> There is a vitality, a life force, energy, a quickening, that is translated through you into action. And because there is only one of you in all time, this expression is unique. And if you block it, it will never exist through any other media. The world will not have it.
>
> It is not your business to determine how good it [your energy] is, nor how valuable, nor how it compares with other expressions. It is your business to keep it yours— clearly and directly, to keep the channel open.

Nelson Mandela, the first black prime minister of South Africa, in his 1994 Inauguration Speech, when he spoke on this topic of being authentic, choose to quote the words of Marianne Williamson in *A Return to Love:*

> Our deepest fear is not that we are inadequate. Our deepest fear is that we are powerful beyond measure. It is our light, not our darkness, that most frightens us. We ask ourselves, "Who am I to be brilliant, gorgeous, talented, and fabulous?" Actually, who are you not to be? You are a child of God. Your playing small doesn't serve the world. There is nothing enlightened about shrinking so that other people won't feel insecure around you. We were born to make manifest the glory of God that is within us. It's not just in some of us; it's in everyone. And as we let our own light shine, we unconsciously give other people permission to do the same. As we are liberated from our own fear, our presence automatically liberates others.

You certainly do not need to be famous—or even an outstanding speaker or writer or dancer—to find your own voice and start to use it. But you will likely have to conquer your fears about letting that voice out, just as Graham talks about and Mandela, using Williamson's words, urges us to do. Once you do, well, who knows?

Chapter 3

FINDING AND WRITING YOUR STORY

Standing Out

I have attended hundreds of college information sessions. These sessions typically precede or follow college tours. Often at these sessions the speaker for the college asks potential applicants what they are interested in studying. Even more often, the speaker tells the audience what influences the admissions committee when it reads student applications. Recently, at one Midwestern campus, in a special information session just for counselors, a college spokesperson said, "We are not looking to accept just one kind of student who fits our image of the perfect student for our campus."

This is contrary to what many students and parents think. They think colleges are looking for well-rounded students who fit a specified mold—one that the college views as ideal. What is more true is that colleges are looking for individual students with individual passions, backgrounds and personal characteristics, who together with other students with different individual passions and characteristics will form a college class possessing many diverse interests and talents. Thus, many individuals contribute to a well-rounded "class" of students.

The spokesperson went on to say that the essay is one of the main methods admissions offices use for distinguishing one student from another. Yet, when an admissions counselor reads the same kind of essays over and over, and each essay says the same things, it makes it difficult to use this tool to decide whom to admit. Parke Muth says this in giving his advice on the University of Virginia website, "We are not looking for students who all think the same way, believe the same thing or write the same essay."

Thus, we are back to the importance of the essay. Your essay matters to colleges selecting students to form a class. So your essay needs to be distinctive. We have seen that an authentic voice is important. Now, how important is good storytelling?

Why Tell a Story?

One thing we have not emphasized enough is why storytelling has such a big impact. Why is it such an effective way of presenting information? Stories are more engaging than facts and lists. Stories form connections between you and your reader. You share your experiences and the reader relates to them, thinking of connections to his or her own experiences. If a reader can sense a connection between the two of you, the reader is more engaged.

Storytelling also makes information easier to understand, and easier to remember. It has also been suggested that we trust story tellers more. Maybe they remind us of our mothers and fathers reading to us when we were too young to read for ourselves. You remember, "Once upon a time …" So, as far as appealing to the reader of your essay, storytelling will make you: more engaging, easier to understand, more memorable, and more trustworthy—all good things.

So what story will you tell to distinguish who you are, and how you interact with your world? I am sure you already have some idea of who you are. Of course, you should start there. What should you do, however, if nothing comes readily to mind?

Finding Your Story

When my students and I begin to brainstorm for the college essay, we often start with a list of characteristics. (Originally I generated this list to help students when a local high school guidance department started asking students to come up with three adjectives to describe themselves.) To start the essay process, I ask the students to circle all the characteristics that they think apply to them. (See Appendix A: **Who Are You?)**

Usually each student will check off a large list of characteristics. Some of these will overlap. I then ask for a narrowed-down list of three or four items that seem strong or relevant. After that the story-telling begins.

"Tell me about a time that shows you were like that." I say. Sometimes students tell a story that shows how they are like that, and sometimes the story they tell just turns into a great story— so we go on to analyze how this story might reveal their values or goals, or perspectives on life. Then I usually say things like, "Are there any other things or stories that come to mind that reflect the same kind of thinking or values?" Essentially, we have a conversation. (Look at the list in Appendix A, now. Choose your list of characteristics. Now see if you can come up with some stories that demonstrate your most significant characteristics or values. Do you like the stories that come to mind?)

Also remember that it is the genuine, authentic quality of an imaginary conversation with me or someone else who wishes all the best for you, that you should maintain when you sit down to write your essay. Forget about your anxiety over the admissions counselor who will be reading your essay. Pretend. Tell your story as if you're talking to your favorite aunt, or uncle—and the counselor will "hear" the authenticity of your voice and your story in the writing you produce.

As you take stock of yourself and your life, you might also think about how the world views you. What adjectives might your parents, siblings, teachers and friends use to describe you? What stories would they tell about you? Would you tell the stories the same way? Why or why not?

Here is part of a story told by an applicant named Kelly. It is based on the view of her assistant basketball coach who saw her slacking off in a game, and this incident and what she took from it, became part of her college essay (This piece has a title, but not all essays need to have or do have one):

A Good Coach Tells You When to Sit up Straight

Nice guys don't make good coaches. A good coach is someone who is passionate, and lets it get the best of him once in a while. I know this because I've had two very different types of coaches.

It was the second game of the season. First quarter, I had been playing well and had already scored 10 points. I had dropped two three-pointers from the same spot within the first two minutes. The second quarter was just beginning and I was still playing well, but did not think so at the time. I had missed a couple shots and was getting extremely aggravated. Once the ball had gone out of bounds I ran over to my bench and asked to be taken out. The head coach, showing no reluctance, took me out immediately, and I went to go cool off on the bench. I was just taking my first sip of water when Coach O'Connell, the assistant coach, walked down from the end of the bench to where I was sitting. Suddenly, he was screaming at me. The whole gym had gone silent and all you could hear was the basketball hitting the floor and the hoop. Everyone stared.

"Why did you ask to come out of the game!?" he screamed at me. "Because I was playing badly," I muttered back. "You never, never, never ask to come out of a game. It is a PRIVILEGE to play on that court. You're lucky I'm not the head coach or I would have you in your street clothes over there with all those hooligans!" He pointed at the bleachers. I couldn't have been more embarrassed.

It wasn't over yet, though. As I was contemplating all this in my head, Coach O'Connell was back in my face yelling at me for something else: "Sit up straight!" Apparently my upper body wasn't erect enough for him.

And this essay goes on to talk about Kelly's renewed dedication to basketball and personal discipline. In this part of the story we see how much Kelly cares about basketball. More importantly, though, we also see that her self-confidence and her love of the game are great—so great that even when her coach embarrasses her, she appreciates his caring about the game more than she worries about being publicly humiliated. This story reveals it all.

If this approach doesn't seem as if it will work for you, here is a slightly different way to use your individual qualities to find your story. Donna Kelly, a friend and colleague who is a college admissions counselor from Minnesota, tells her students to imagine that they are only allowed to send in three things in support of their application for admissions. These are: a transcript, an ACT or SAT scores, and a piece of paper with three words on it. What should those words be for you? Think about how the qualities represented by these words can be illustrated. This can lead to some good storytelling and will provide the seeds of a good essay.

One other piece of advice that Donna gives her students is advice she heard from a college admissions officer; he said something to the effect of, "Don't write about world peace— just tell me what's on your nightstand." This further advice, again, reinforces the goals of striving to be authentic, genuine, and natural, and to talk about what you yourself know about life.

Challenges, Setbacks, and Making a Difference

Other times, in finding your story, it is helpful to distinguish who you are by asking yourself some big questions, questions such as: What setbacks have I had? What have I learned from a bad situation or mistake? (See Appendix B: **What Has Happened to You?**)

One college has done some impressive thinking about topics such as these, topics which make for good insights about applicants. Oregon State University's admissions officers have generated a fascinating list of six questions any one of which, by itself, could serve as the stimulus for a thoughtful essay. See "Insight Resume" at**http://oregonstate.edu/admissions/publications/insight_res ume_worksheet.pdf.**

Applicants to OSU are asked to answer all six of these questions and instructed to use no more than 100 words for each answer. This alone calls for careful thought and great economy of expression. To give you an idea of the nature of the questions, let me describe one. OSU asks a student to comment on the most significant challenge he or she has faced and the steps the student has taken to address this challenge. It asks the student to include, in the answer, whether he or she has turned to anyone in facing the challenge, the role that person played, and what the student learned about him or herself. Another of the six questions asks students to explain what they have done to make their community a better place to live. It asks for examples of specific projects in which they have been involved over time.

OSU explains on its Web site why the answers to these thought-provoking questions will help them understand who you, the applicant, are. The Web site states:

The insight resume gives us an understanding of you as a unique, contributing individual, an understanding of your accomplishments, perspectives, experiences, and talents, your achievements within the context of your social and personal circumstances, and how participation in activities has developed academic, intellectual, and leadership abilities.

When you tell such a story, the kind of story you will tell in discussing a significant challenge you have faced, for example, can make you stand out by showing how you handled such a setback. One student, a few years ago, talked about how a challenge within the family when her dad lost his job turned into an opportunity for her.

You Can't Make a Whole Lot of Noise If You Want to Catch Anything

A few years ago I never would have thought I'd be fly fishing with my dad. My dad wasn't around all that often with his busy job and traveling. I didn't mind it when he would go on business trips; I was actually quite used to it. Almost the only time I saw him was when I would come home from lacrosse practice in the spring; he and my mom would be in the kitchen discussing their day over a glass of wine. But when he lost his job a couple of summers ago everything changed. We had a lot more time to do things as a family… My dad discovered fly fishing when he wandered into the Orvis store next to Trader Joes where he would shop for groceries. My mom and my sister both showed an extreme lack of enthusiasm when he presented the new hobby to them. I wasn't exactly thrilled about it either, but since I was the youngest I was pressured to give it a try…. my dad and I shared laughs over our few catches that were never larger than five to six inches in length.

Talking wasn't necessary because we both appreciated the sounds of rapids and birds chirping all around us. Fishing was a huge bonding experience; it has definitely brought us closer together.... I picked up some new skills and stories that helped our relationship grow stronger when we went fishing. It's not that I was happy my dad lost his job, but I am happy I got to spend time with him.

Here is the beginning of another story by a student who reveals how her personal philosophy in life usually allowed her to see any negative situation in a positive light:

I Like It When the Flowers Break

The endless boxes of flowers that I unloaded from the truck were heavy and so dirty my clothes always showed a hard day's work. I'd walk back and forth from the truck to the benches, carrying as many boxes as I could manage at a time. When finally the truck was emptied, and more than one hundred boxes had been stacked around the benches, it was time to get to work.

I kept my tools handy in my back pocket: a paring knife, leaf strippers, and clippers. It was my job to open the boxes, cut all the stems off the flowers, remove a certain amount of foliage, place all the flowers in buckets of treated water, and move all the buckets into the refrigerator. All this work had to be done with the utmost attention to detail and delicate care so as to not damage any of the flowers. But sometimes the flowers were broken when I opened the box, and sometimes they broke no matter how careful I tried to be. This made me sad. But when that happened, I got to take the flowers home. The flowers were rendered useless to the florists, but to me they were beautiful.

How Are You Different?

Now, let us consider another possible essay approach: how do you differ from your peers? This is the approach that Olga, from Chapter 1, used. When I discuss this "how am I unique?" kind of response with students I always tell a story about myself. I tell a story about body surfing—not so much because it makes me unique, but because it is something I know very well. It also provides a metaphor for life. When you body surf you have to know what to do when the waves come in, sometimes these waves are good ones for riding into the beach and sometimes they are just too weak to be worth catching. Sometimes, though, they are very strong, and you are just in the wrong place when the wave catches you! How should you react then? If a wave is bearing down on you, you have to dive into or through it. You can't swim away and you can't float over it, so you have to do what seems almost counter-intuitive; you have to dive right into it! If you float or try to stand, the wave will rough you up, knock you down and pound you into the sand on floor of the ocean. In life, sometimes, diving right into that which you fear is the best way to respond.

I once helped a student named David who was having a tough time beginning his essay. All he could think of as a topic for an essay that could distinguish him from others was his role on the football team. Then I asked him about his life guarding job. What are the skills you need to rescue someone from the ocean? What kind of preparation do the lifeguards do to stay in shape? And what is the most difficult situation you have faced?

Grinning, David explained that the toughest situation the lifeguards faced on a daily basis, other than standing ready to rescue a swimmer, were the situation caused by the presence of jelly fish in the water. David was amused while sharing how the guards always had a tough time explaining to parents about the various antidotes for jelly fish stings. Here is what David wrote:

The way to tell how "serious" a jelly fish sting a child has suffered is by the ratio of how old the kid is, to how much he's screaming, to how much his parents are worried about it. If you get a three-year-old who is tearing up and holding his or her mother's hand, and the parent is only mildly concerned, it's not that big of a deal. If, however, it's an eight-year-old kid who's screaming like he's been shot and he is being carried in his father's arms—yes, this has happened—it's a much bigger deal.

…Your first attempt at a cure, though, should be wet sand and salt water. If you rub the sand in one direction over the sting you can get most of the barbs out. Most people look at you in shock and amazement when you tell them this. You can just picture what goes through the adult's mind, "He must be kidding," or "Is he qualified to work here?" or "Is he serious; my little Johnny here is writhing in pain and this imbecile wants to put sand on it?!" If that treatment doesn't work, then we have vinegar in the lifeguard shack. After applying the vinegar, or "Jelly Juice," as the lifeguards like to call it, if little Johnny is still crying, we have one last line of defense. This has yet to fail.

Urine stops the pain almost instantly and sooths the sting on contact. It can smell, but no more than the Jelly Juice does. This means taking Johnny to the bathroom and having him pee in a cup which the mom had commandeered from the eating establishment next door and then using a gauze pad to apply, liberally I might add, the urine to the area that had been stung…

The interesting thing about this story, which continued on, is that it showed that the student knew how to size up people, and also had a sense of humor, but it didn't even mention, although it suggests by implication, two other characteristics that are very important to his job: a commitment to be physically fit enough to rescue a swimmer, through tough ocean workouts, and a willingness to take on the serious risk of performing a sea rescue. This is a great story. It also introduces a concern and suggests a word of caution about subject matter, however. As one admission's counselor said, "Don't try to shock us. Believe me, we have read it all."

Beginning Your Story with a Teaser

Starting your story with a few sentences that capture your reader's attention creates more of an impact than starting at the beginning of the story and proceeding. English teachers sometimes call this attention-getting opening a hook, a teaser or a zinger. Often a story told in this fashion begins in the middle, and then fills in the beginning, and finishes with a final resolution. Typically the opening sentence references a surprising moment in the story, or some interesting dialogue, or a thought that sounds paradoxical at first glance. This introductory moment or snippet of dialogue is not entirely explained or understood until the story finally reaches its conclusion.

This approach gives you more of a chance to grab the reader's attention than otherwise. Admissions counselors review approximately 30 student applications a day. Seven hundred applications during the reading season of the year is a light load for a counselor. A more usual load, especially at a large university, would be 1,000 to 1,200 applications. So you want your story to be an immediate attention-getter. How better to ensure this than by starting your essay with a zinger? When I explain this technique to students, I sometimes use this example.

Suppose the essay you were reading started like this? "I was getting ready to steal. You would think I would be used to it by now, but every time I do it, my palms get sweaty, my stomach ties itself in knots, and it is hard to breathe. Finally I see my moment." As the reader what would you be thinking after these first three lines? Does this student know what he is doing? The student can't be going to describe a crime; this is his college essay. The fourth sentence or maybe some other sentence even further into the essay would likely state, "Digging in my cleats, I began sprinting for second base." Clearly as the reader you would have been engaged.

Thinking about this technique, let's consider some first lines (you will find out how a few of these essays actually develop in the next chapter):

- All official documents will tell you that I am one of five children. They will tell you that I have two brothers and two sisters. But that is not the case. I have a third sister.

- I was late for work— I had overslept. It was the first day of a summer-long internship at the *Wilton Villager* and I was scheduled to meet with the editor-in-chief over a cup of coffee.

- By the time I got to high school, I was accustomed to coasting.

- I studied for my AP U.S. History exam by sleeping twenty hours a day, watching television when I did wake up, and fasting for three weeks.

- "An inch too short. A step to slow." is what I hear. I am standing outside Coach Marinelli's office and I hear these words uttered, as one college coach after another assesses the 5'11" stocky kid in the red number 55 jersey, who fills the TV screen.

- Every year Sandy sends me a birthday card, buys me a Christmas present and sends me inspirational excerpts from the Bible even though she knows I don't believe in God.

- I am floating on a yellow life jacket with only clear water surrounding me and a metal bowl of dishes bobbing a few feet away.

- Rain is blinding us, and our feet keep slipping on the wet, muddy ground. But still we run on. Me and John. John and me. Sprinting faster and faster.

- As fate would have it, my broken back brought Eric and me together. Eric is awkward, tall, skinny, and has the athletic ability of a rock. Eric is also hardworking, determined, and a great learner.

Inspiration from Other Effective Story Tellers

There are several other resources that I think you should know about and which will provide you with inspiration, as well as examples of effective storytelling. One place where you can see stories that are effective is at a Web site for a National Public Radio Station program called *This I Believe* (http://thisibelieve.org/essaywritingtips.html).

The instructions for submitting stories to *This I Believe* might prove useful to you in thinking about effective essay writing. This show invites listeners to share their values with the station's audience by using stories to illustrate them. The instructions for the essay (350 to 500 words), which the listener-writer will ultimately be reading on the air, are to tell a story which only he or she can tell and to illustrate beliefs using the events of his or her life. Expressed another way, the listener (referred to as you) is (are) invited to talk about the value or values that govern your thoughts and actions.

Significantly, the instructions also tell you to read your essay aloud several times and to edit it each time until you find that the words, tone and story "echo the way you speak." This is also very good advice to follow when writing your college essay. Your essay will sound more and more like you; you will be able to identify any words not in your normal vocabulary, if you read the essay aloud and continue to simplify it. You can find some good stories on the Web site of *This I Believe* (http://thisibelieve.org/dsp_Browse.php) including examples of stories that have engaged listeners and proved distinctive. In fact, maybe you can submit your completed college essay to *This I Believe,* as well as to the admissions office.

Let's talk about another place where the instructions given for story telling could prove insightful if applied to the college essay. During the Presidential Campaign of 2008, Obama organizers, in their early grass-roots stage, asked attendees at regional meetings called "camps" to tell each other their life stories following a format developed by Harvard professor Marshall Ganz.

Using his college experience Professor Ganz (http://www.hks.harvard.edu/about/faculty-staff-directory/marshall-ganz), modeled the format for the exercises he presented at these gatherings on a course he teaches at Harvard calls "Public Narrative." (To get a feel for the course, visit this Web site: ttp://www.hks.harvard.edu/degrees/teaching-and-courses/courses/public-narrative-conflict-collaboration-and-coherence.)

Ganz had originally been inspired by the personal stories of other participants during the "Freedom Summer" of the Civil Rights Movement. During that summer of 1964 as he listened to the stories of other participants, he felt moved by their power and hope. The goal of his course at Harvard is to teach more people how to tell their life stories.

Such a story, according to Ganz, has three parts—the story of "self," which should communicate who you are; the story of "us," which should explain your values and the groups you make part of your life; and the story of "now," which should explain what—if the present moment is considered one of choice and hope—you see as important to accomplish.

I think that the personal college admissions essay may be approached in almost the same way. I believe you will find Ganz's discussion questions may inspire you to do the deep kind of thinking a personal essay sometimes elicits and often expects. And you will distinguish yourself in the writing of it the more you connect with your reader and the harder you look into your "why and how," as you explore this defining moment of change in your life—identifying your hopes as you go off to college. Your vision of what you can accomplish may not be fully formed, but your consideration of its possibilities may have an impact when shared with your reader.

A final example of effective story telling that you might examine is a speech given by Steve Jobs, the founder and CEO of Pixar Animation Studios and Apple Computer to the Stanford University graduating class in 2005. I have shared the text of Steve Jobs' commencement address (Here is the Web address of both a text and a video version of the commencement speech: http://news.stanford.edu/news/2005/june15/jobs-061505.) with all my student writers, and even though they are reading it and not hearing it, none of them ever looks up—except at the very end, when they say, "Wow!"

How does Steve achieve such a response? When he begins to talk, he informs the listeners that he just wants to tell three stories. All of the listeners (and, by now, we feel as if we are part of this audience) are already anticipating stories about an extra-ordinary life, as the founder of both Apple Computer and Pixar Animation Studios. Also we are already comfortable that he is talking to us and not over us—almost like a conversation. Then he ensures our complete attention by telling us that we will not be able to identify his full purpose until the end of the speech— just as he was not able to anticipate the way his life's course would unfold as he moved forward through time. His final words not only tie his stories and his speech together, but they magically, also serve to communicate his advice to the graduates. As a masterful use of both storytelling and voice, this speech also exemplifies, on a grander scale what an effective admissions essay might accomplish.

Length of Your Essay

We have not yet talked about the length of your personal college essay and I know that sometimes students worry about this. So before you begin reading the wonderful students essays in Chapter 4, I think that we should discuss the length of college essays. You will see that some of the essays in this section are longer than 500 words. On the other hand, I have had students submit fine essays that were less than 300 words. For many years the instructions on the Common Application, both before it was online and since it has been online, specified a personal essay of no longer than 500 words. However, recently the space allocated for the upload of the essay has been changed so that essays of longer lengths may be submitted. This was done to allow all students who feel they need more space to take it. However, I still think the wise thing to do is to be mindful of the 30 applications per day that college admissions counselors are said to read. I would try to limit my words to around 500, as long as doing so does not cramp your story or your style. On the other hand, if your essay is marvelously interesting and you think the counselor will want to read it, even if it is the last application of the day, and it is longer than 500 words, don't spoil it by cutting.

Chapter 4

MEMORABLE ESSAYS: HOW, WHY, WHERE THEY WORKED

This chapter contains thirteen student essays. The essays are organized in groups to help you understand that each student author had to work through the essay writing process in a slightly different way. I've also prefaced each essay with my thoughts about why and how the essay was successful for me. You'll find my comments in italics.

Besides being great stories and good essays, Essays 1, 2 and 3 are important as illustrations of what can come from doing some intense brain storming. At first Essay 2 simply refused to unfold as a story. The student knew she wanted to write about the summer of her life, when she had felt free, but she couldn't figure out how to compress and focus her thoughts. It was almost as if the summer was too wonderful to be captured in words. Finally I said to her: "Don't try to tell the whole story, just put down a few lines about the little things you remember feeling." Essay 2 resulted—this was the story she had wanted to share.

The kind of brainstorming that went into Essays 1 and 3 illustrates other issues. The author of Essay 1 knew she wanted to tell her story but she couldn't get it on paper. Perhaps, it was too emotional. One day she told it to me out loud, sentence by sentence. After each sentence she typed the words. Then I would say, "What happened next?" The student who wrote Essay 3 had his title and first paragraph for more than a month, but he couldn't seem to go on—he overcame this block one afternoon when he wrestled the specific into sentences.

Essays 4, 5 and 6 illustrate how to use significant details and dialogue to show rather than tell the reader what is happening.

Also don't let anybody edit out important details (Essay 4). If you have a good-natured humorous take on the world, let it come out (Essay 5). Finally don't hesitate to talk about your grandparents if you know this is significant (Essay 6).

Essays 7, 8 and 9 illustrate how important it is to use your authentic voice. Your purpose is to tell a story—frame an essay—that, as Mark, my student, said earlier, "is so you!" Be sure to write in the voice you feel is authentic, no matter how quiet (Essay 8) or bold (Essay 9) this may seem.

Essay 7 evolved after a student suggested to me that she wanted her personal college essay to be about an important medical event in her life. Whenever my students tells me they want to write about some illness or physical hardship that they have endured, I always ask them "Does this define you as a person or will this be just the story of you as survivor?" Such hardships may be a part of who you are and the frailty you felt may have influenced your life for a time, but don't more lasting traits and values define who you are? Did these emerge or stay strong during the difficulty? Once her story focused on revealing something of the person she was, the student wrote Essay 7. Her voice is wonderful.

Essays 10, 11, and 12 illustrate again how fine a story can be told through the skillful use of details and description. While Essays 10 and 12 flow along effortlessly, Essay 11 does have some problems. The action part of Essay 11 is great—with the writer using internal dialogue and action verbs to capture the action, but in parts two and three of the essay the writer engages some difficult and pithy philosophical topics. In these parts, the essay slows down, but it never stops reporting the inner dialogue of the writer and the writer never loses his voice. See what you think.

Essay 13 illustrates the kind of essay I told you is not strictly considered a personal essay. However, in case you have to write this kind of essay, here is a good example of how a student can maintain voice, even when writing a "supplemental" why-do-you-want-to-come-to-our-college essay.

Essay 1

I always figure it is a pretty safe bet that if I cry reading a student's personal essay, the student has an effective piece that will also touch a college admissions officer. Even though I have been through the brain-storming and revising processes during the essay's writing, on the day that the piece is finally done and gets presented to me for a final read, I often try to forget the other times I have seen the piece. Then the genuine feelings and intention that come across are very intense. My students always kid me that, "You know it's good if she cries." This essay made me cry. The voice of the writer is strong, compassionate, and unabashedly straightforward. It indicates a mature young woman who has taken on the nurturing of another woman—an older woman—because she feels it is something she ought to do. Surely this is the kind of soul whose presence would enrich a campus.

I want to say a word about the process of how this essay came to be. The student had struggled for many weeks to write this essay that she felt reflected her real self and meant a great deal to her. We had been though the brain-storming process many times. She also had told me many other stories. Each week she would write another essay, one about track, one about being an actor, one about a good friend, but none was the right story, she said. She had told me the general story of Jerry early on, but she hadn't felt she had the words to write it. Finally one day I thought we knew each other well enough to ask her to tell me in detail how it had happened. First, she told me about being on the computer and receiving the instant message. I told her to stop and write that down. She went on; each time she told me another part of the story, I had her write it down. The part of

49

the story that is first in the essay was actually the last thing she told me. The order of the story in the final essay was used for dramatic effect. I think there is a lesson, though, in the process she used. If you feel you are stuck, one thought is to tell your story aloud to someone else. If you don't think you have a listener you trust, perhaps you could say it aloud and record it. The student was accepted, early decision, to Trinity University in Connecticut.

Sandy Eckles

Every year Sandy sends me a birthday card, buys me a Christmas present and sends me inspirational excerpts from the Bible even though she knows I don't believe in God. Every day after school she "instant messages" me to find out how I am, and within the first hundred words she says, "It's so nice to know what Jerry would be doing now." She asks me about school, sports, theatre, and even the sensitive topic of college. She keeps me up to date on all the whereabouts of my Texas friends, and I inform her of various matters in my own life.

Sandy is the mother of Jerry, and Jerry was my best friend from age eight until he died when I was fifteen— just as we were both beginning our first year of high school. January twenty-first, a Friday afternoon, I was sitting in front of my laptop, typing away to friends when I received the worst news of my young life through means of instant message. I sat there emotionless, unsure of what to do. I just sat wide-eyed taking in my room around me. I could only think about his mother, how she must have felt when she received the phone call that her son had fallen dead on a youth group trip, and wondered why God would want to take his soul so young? I took out a pen and a piece of my monogrammed stationary, and began to write, "Dear

50

Mrs. Eckles, I loved your son." I couldn't think of what else to write. These were the only rational words that came to mind. I put my completed letter in the mail, and broke down.

I knew how much I loved him, and all I could think about was how his mother was going to say goodbye to him. She knew him eight years longer than I did, and loved him for those eight years more, as well. I didn't know her very well. I only knew her from the Episcopal School book fair. Nevertheless I wanted to send her flowers, because I thought it would be a good thing to do.

Our relationship began a few weeks later. Just as I was getting into the shower, an instant message appeared on my screen from Jerry's screen name. For a moment, I believed he was still alive and talking to me and his death was just a huge joke. Though, the next IM popped up saying, "Hi. It is Sandy. I just wanted to thank you for the beautiful flowers and letter you sent." I hated her. Everything about her reminded me of Jerry and all I wanted to do was forget and move on with my life. I couldn't even make myself respond.

Now, three years later, I have a second mother, and I tell her a lot of things I would never tell my real mother, because she would kill me. I expect to be lifelong friends, and next year while sitting in my freshman dorm room, Sandy will be asking me how my first days of classes have gone and if I have met any cute boys.

They say that everything happens for a reason, and we'll be better people when we're through it. Although, I am still waiting to see how this relationship will unfold in the long run, I can confidently say, that Sandy has helped me in more ways than just getting through my best friend's death and I know that I have been a supporting spirit in her life for the last three years.

Essay 2

The student who wrote the following story was the most socially capable student I have ever had as a client. She brought people together into groups. Kids felt good about themselves as they accomplished cooperative tasks. In the tenth grade, after being shown the film The Hotel Rwanda, this student organized speakers who came to visit the high school to speak about Darfur. She then initiated a fund raiser to support Darfur's refugees. She was also an accomplished sailor, and knew that the sea helped her recover her energy. The following essay combines both aspects of her life and is about a group sailing trip between her junior and senior year during which she became, as you might expect, the boat's "mother." The story is told in snippets of action and reflection, not as a coherent story. The very style of this essay reveals the student's openness and spontaneity. And like the style, all of her reflections seem open and genuine. This student attended Boston University.

My Passion Is the Sea

I am floating on a yellow life jacket with only clear blue water surrounding me and a metal bowl of dishes bobbling a foot away. Everyone else is cleaning dishes over the side, but this morning I went swimming before everyone else. So prepared with my scrubber in hand I am cleaning my dishes in the middle of the ocean. A sea turtle swims underneath, close enough to reach with my toes. I am living on the *Arwen*, a 50-foot sloop rigged sailboat with 12 strangers in the middle of the Eastern Caribbean. The wind and the sea are our only power.

We have only been at sea for three weeks and in these days and nights I have already begun to see the ocean becoming a part of me. I've been around boats since before I could walk, always living within 20 minutes of the shore, but never had I been close enough to really be a part of it. Not until now.

The first night, I open my eyes to a glimmering ocean, lit by a starry night. Where am I? Quickly I turn to the left and see that I am still on the boat. We are sardines in our sleeping bags, across the bow, up the deck, even inside the sails. The only thing between us and falling into the ocean is a 2-inch fiberglass ridge and a flimsy row of safety lines encircling the boat. It is hard to sleep when you are living in a dream.

After being at sea for less than a week, I am sold to the salty blue sea. Every time the boat stops we fearlessly jump off the stern and swim to the neighboring sailboats and even to land. For the first time I feel no fear.

At sunrise we leave the boat to hike 12 miles through the rainforest, across the valley of desolation, and up into the clouds, finally to see a murky lake of boiling water that smells like egg salad. It is one of the hardest things I have ever done, but I would do it again.

On this evening we will anchor late. I zip up my spray jacket to block the salty smacks as we cut through the waves. The sun is setting on our evening sail and the wind is getting cool. It is getting harder to see, but we keep on moving. We have to get to our anchorage. Everyone in the cockpit is sleeping. There are only a few left still awake... I am sitting on the port side of the stern, drenched in sea water. Another wave splashes over. It twitches and flaps. A flying fish is in my lap. I've caught a fish. Me!

On the fourth week I am asked to teach a group of younger high schoolers to sail the 50-foot sailboat. I am intimidated at first but I accept the challenge. I take out the whiteboard and explain the different points of sail and parts of the sailboat. We learn how to use the wind to our advantage. The day goes by relatively smoothly. I think, "This is something I could get used to." As we pull into our anchorage I assign all the kids their last job of the day. One in particular is to hold the dinghy line so it does not get caught in the propellers when we turn the engine on to drop anchor—a simple task that I had watched happen almost every day for a month. As we wait for the anchor to hit the bottom and catch, the helmsman switches the boat into reverse. With my back to the stern of the boat I do not see, but we hear the large splash. I turn around to see the girl with the dingy line in the water holding on to the back of the boat as her legs start to get pulled underneath the boat. It is a split second out of a horror scene and I think fast. "Put the engine in neutral," I shout to the helmsman, while I jump down to grab the girl's hand. We pull her back onto the boat completely unscratched. I sit down to breathe as everyone rushes around me. I think I'm starting to get gray hairs.

I wake up on a rainy morning at 5:30, ready to catch the taxi to Brother Kings Turtle Sanctuary. With rain gear and scrub brushes at hand, we are ready to work. I help to chop the fish into bite-sized pieces for the hundreds of turtles surrounding me. Then it is time to give them a scrub and clean their tanks. I clean the baby sea turtles, nearly five weeks old, with toothbrushes as they squirm in my hands. In four years they will be large enough to return to the sea. By the time we are ready to leave, our bodies and clothes are completely splattered with green algae. I do not say goodbye to my new friends because I know that in five years or maybe in twenty, I will reunite with one of my turtles swimming free as I sail around the world.

The sea has taught me to be brave, unpredictable, fearless, forgiving, strong, motherly, calm, and independent. It has taught me to be me.

Essay 3

When I suggest you tell your stories as if you are talking to someone you trust, I can't help thinking about an essay written by a student who longed to be able to play football in college, but feared coaches might not recognize his talent. Still he didn't hesitate to address this concern--and confront his worst fears—while confiding in the reader of his essay. Because he treats the reader as if he or she were a friend, clearly on his side, because this *student knows that his confidence in facing reality and his strength as a leader are obvious, and because he knows it is a great hook, this story teller uses the name of his essay, "An Inch Too Short...A Step Too Slow" as an early indicator of his dilemma. Also notice the student's use of detail in the first scene. I feel as though I am standing in the hall with him. The one problem with the essay occurs in the second half. The essay loses its conversational flow and starts to do more telling than showing. Not keeping* one's *voice consistent is often a challenge to new writers. See if you notice this. Finally, we should recognize that, although this essay is about sports, not a very distinctive topic as college essays go, I have to think that this particular perspective and especially this voice is not that common. This student was recruited to play football at and attended Bowdoin College in Maine.*

"An Inch Too Short. A Step Too Slow. "

I am standing outside Coach Marinelli's office, and I hear these words uttered, as one college coach after another assesses the 5'11" stocky kid wearing the red number 55 jersey, who fills the TV screen. As they watch film of me making plays, they can see right away that I am not the prototypical 6'5" behemoth that they are looking for to fill out their lines. But this is not the first time in my life that I have heard words similar to these. And at 5'11" I have always striven harder than most to be better than most.

I think what separates me from the massive pack of high school students is my perseverance in overcoming any disadvantage. After identifying any strengths and weaknesses, I have always formulated a plan of attack. So even though I know that I am an inch too short and a step too slow to initially show up on a major college coach's radar, I know that through weight-training and positive thinking, I have overcome these apparent shortcomings.

Now, I know what you are thinking. "Oh no, here goes another kid with a football story." But what I want to show you next is how I have used this same approach to bring about other changes in my high school experience.

At New Canaan High School, I have also found ways to be a difference maker by trying harder and being positive. I believe that I am able to contribute service to my community by using my position as football captain. By way of my position, I have the respect of not only my teammates, but the entire student body. So in this position, I take it upon myself to remedy some of the injustice that occurs around me. One instance in which I did this was in the school library, when I saw two bullies chasing around one of my younger teammates. He was a foreign exchange student still trying to assimilate to American ways. But all of a sudden, the librarian decided to discipline my teammate, who was actually a victim of the bullying. Seeing this situation unfold, I went up to the librarian, and told her to not reprimand my teammate, but instead punish the others. Back on the football field, I use my position to convince the younger players to believe in themselves. For example, if I see a younger player struggle through the drills, I will take him aside, and work with him until he is comfortable.

By accepting myself for what I am, I can be genuine with people, and let them see me for what I truly am. Without giving into bravado, chauvinism, and all of those false facades, I can let people see the values with which I govern my life.

Essay 4

I always tell my students to try not to let an editor or an anxious parent change their finished essay. At a recent admissions office talk with counselors, an admissions counselor went so far as to say that students shouldn't let either their parents or their English teacher see their essay. "They will edit the voice out of it." Of course, it is a good thing to have a second pair of eyes point out grammatical or logic errors, but students should avoid letting parents take out details that "make you look bad," or add things because, "maybe the person reading this didn't see all your A's and might not realize what a hard worker you are." Often the details that parents want to take out are the very ones that give the student an authentic voice and make him or her *seem human. In the case of the following story, the growth, understanding, and camaraderie attained by the student as he matured through his summer experience would have been less obvious, had* he removed *the first paragraph (His mother suggested this because she thought being late for work would reflect badly on him.) This student attended George Washington University in Washington, DC.*

I was late for work—I had overslept. It was the first day of a summer-long internship at the *Wilton Villager* and I was scheduled to meet with the editor-in-chief over a cup of coffee in a half-hour. Driving as fast as a new driver possibly can (I had been a licensed driver for eight days at that point), I arrived at the *Villager*'s offices just 10 minutes late. But where were all the cars? Only one car was parked in the lot in front of the building. Had I gone to the wrong place? Did I write down the wrong time? I cautiously approached the front door. Pulling it open ever so slightly, I crept inside to find a bearded man sitting at the reception desk.

"Good morning Jonathan!" he cheerfully exclaimed, as only a heavily caffeinated man could at 8:45 in the morning. "I'm Alex, the photographer, everyone else should be here in a little while," he said. Sure enough, by 9:30 or so, the staff of six had sauntered into the offices. Donna, the editor-in-chief, cheerfully called me into her office just a few minutes after she arrived.

"I'm sorry I was late this morning," I whispered, not having the courage to speak any louder. Donna laughed. It was then that I realized how laid back a weekly newspaper really is.

Three days later, I found myself across the street, at the hair salon where I would conduct my first interview as a "professional" journalist. Introducing myself as a reporter from the *Villager*, I felt an unfamiliar sense of admiration from the staff and patrons of the salon, who looked at me with a sense of awe. It might have been this very moment that made me realize how much power a journalist has in a democratic society.

When I arrived in the newsroom on the day of publication, I rushed for the first newspaper I could find. Looking frantically for my article on Page 2, or 7, or 10, I could not find it. Heartbroken, afraid that the editors had decided that my work didn't quite meet the mark of professional journalism, I turned back to the front cover to read the rest of the news. A picture of a young girl caught my eye at the bottom of the page. Wasn't that the girl who had cut her hair for Locks of Love? Suddenly, a byline with my name in it appeared – on the front page! I was at a loss for words.

For the next three months, I wrote news stories, feature stories, sports stories, and a weekly column, "A Teen Perspective." Traveling all over town, I slowly began to learn the rituals and customs of a journalist. Lunch was always eaten over a newspaper; it didn't matter if it was last week's issue of the *Villager* or *The New York Times*. I would never travel anywhere without a reporter's notebook again. I still keep a tape recorder and camera in my car, never knowing when a story might break.

And one day, the story did. In the town of Wilton, a small suburb of just under 20,000 people, front-page headlines are usually devoted to school news, budget cuts or, occasionally, a traffic accident or robbery. One day, breaking news happened. As I walked into the offices one sultry morning, the entire staff was present. Scared that I had overslept, I asked what was going on. The night before, a group of teenagers from a neighboring town had trespassed into a quarry to go swimming. One young man, stuck in the middle and probably caught on one of the vines that grows underneath the surface, drowned in the deep, water-filled chasm. Jerrod, the assistant editor, asked me to accompany him to the scene.

We arrived at a deserted parking lot, overgrown with weeds and tall grass through the cracks of pavement. I had never been around more than one member of the press at a time while working on a story. This time, there were 10. In addition, the local television station had sent not just a news crew, but its helicopter, which was hovering overhead. I was introduced to everyone, who seemed to belong to a social club with each other, somewhat like the White House press corps appears on television.

"You know, Alex should be here," Jerrod said, referring to the *Villager*'s photographer. Then he said the words I had dreaded all along. "I'll be back in 20 minutes," he said. Without waiting for my reply, Jerrod sped off to bring Alex to the scene. Not knowing what to do, I stood by myself, watching the road leading to the quarry where police continuously moved in and out of the site. Several reporters came over to me, to discuss the state of journalism, why they liked working in a smaller market as opposed to a city, and the education a journalist should have. Suddenly I felt comfortable, as if I belonged there. This was tested as Police Officer Isidro, the same man who taught a D.A.R.E. course at my middle school, stepped before the tape recorders and notebooks—and one camera—to address the media.

As I stepped away from what was my first ever press conference, my face glowed with accomplishment. Jerrod's car pulled into the lot. Running towards me, the assistant editor stopped when he saw the look on my face. "I missed it, didn't I?" he said. Laughing, he gave me a pat on the back. When we walked into the newsroom later that morning, it was no longer the assistant editor, the photographer, and the intern. I had joined the club.

Essay 5

The next essay was written by a young man who took on the role of a true mentor by challenging and supporting a depressed friend. He invited the friend on a hair-raising trip into the Alps on bicycles, and then had the unfortunate luck to be physically unable to finish the trip himself. The tables turned, and the friend "paid forward" the favor and became a mentor himself. The voice of the storyteller is humorous, knowing, and happy with himself and life, in general. The twists and turns of the story offer sunny surprises—full of dry humor and wisdom. I can still see the student's smiling eyes, as he first told me this story. He was accepted after applying early decision to Occidental College in California.

Changing Lives

I was getting psyched to go on my summer *Overland* bike trip from London to Rome, but I was really worried about my best friend, Tommy. I knew that his only plans were to sit at home and watch TV. So, with five months left before the trip was scheduled to depart, I picked up the phone and called him. I told him to go buy a bike because we were going to be biking through four countries, for a total of 1500 miles, averaging 80 miles per day. I went on to further warn him that we would be camping every night, and would be living with whatever bare essentials we could carry. I told him if he really wanted to do this, he could, but he would have to start now. I also assured him I'd help him any way I could.

To my surprise he was tentatively open to the idea. "Are you sure I can do it?" he asked incredulously. I could tell from the inflection of his voice that a little push and much support could get him on board. "Of course you can," I replied, "but you're going to need to train hard to get in shape and go on bike rides, some up to 100 miles a day." For a split second we questioned if this would be possible since the last bike he owned had three wheels, and the only sports he played were on *Sony Play Station 2*. In short, he was everything but athletic. "If you persevere, you can do anything," I insisted. Trusting, eager, and committed, within the week Tommy had signed up for the program (a difficulty level 9 out of 10), bought a bike, and signed up for personal training sessions. He had crossed the starting line but had a long race ahead of him.

Tommy trained intensely in the relatively short time he had. I had trained steadily, too, throughout the year, and had biked from Seattle to San Francisco the previous summer without a problem. But we were both apprehensive the night before we left. I reassured him that he had trained harder than anyone else I knew. And if he ever had any trouble, we would stop and take a break together. "You got this made," I said reassuringly. We met each other at the airport with our overstuffed backpacks on our backs and our bikes packed tightly in their boxes, ready to begin our journey.

Three countries and 1,000 miles later, we were on the border of Switzerland and Italy sitting beside our bikes, 8,100 feet above sea level. It was a time to be grateful for our rigorous training days of the past and marvel over all that we had accomplished in the preceding month. We had, that day alone, climbed 14 miles over the Swiss Alps and it seemed as though the rest of the trip was, literally and figuratively, downhill. We celebrated with Pepsis and gelato and started our descent along the mountain switchbacks into Italy, our final destination. Then the trip took an unexpected turn.

My lower spine impacted first as I was projected off my bike at 50 mph. I flipped multiple times and lay there motionless in the middle of the mountain pass. It was a scalding day, easily over 100 degrees Fahrenheit, and the asphalt I lay on was searing my skin. I was staring at the sun. I could move my legs. I wasn't paralyzed. Green Day was blaring through the headphone in my left ear, and I heard calls from behind me through my right. Tommy and our leader, Eric, both of whom had been behind me, rushed to my side. Tommy held a tarp over my mangled body to block the sun. "Alright, what did you do now?" he asked jokingly. It was his turn to be supportive. I couldn't laugh. We looked at each other, knowing that Tommy would have to finish the trip for both of us.

It turned out I fractured my spine in fifteen places and slipped two discs, but today, after seven hours of surgery and six months of physical therapy, I am stronger than ever. Tommy was with me the whole way, sending postcards from Italy, telling me how horrible the last 12 days of the trip were without me, and assuring me that I wasn't missing anything (even though I knew he was lying through his teeth). Also, as soon as he returned home, he stopped in frequently to visit me, and back in school he helped me juggle my backpack with my complex back brace system.

Tommy, the success story, recently completed a triathlon, and placed first in his age group in the Tour de Greenwich thereby qualifying for the "Escape from Alcatraz" triathlon in San Francisco. He says he is in the process of training for an Iron Man competition. I told him he was insane. He simply smiled and replied, "A friend once told me, 'if you persevere, you can do anything,'" I smiled back and said, "See you there."

Essay 6

I think it is important for any group to have a traditionalist, someone who reveres the traditions that are important to the group. This person is the storyteller, the history-keeper who remembers how certain ceremonies are performed *and why they are important. Such a one treasures the traditions of the group and reminds its members of stories of their common past. The student who wrote the story that follows is such a person. She clearly reveres her grandparents and loves her family. She likes to tell the old stories that are family stories, and she shares the values that her family values. She is also well aware, however, of the world around her and the challenges it represents. In this essay we also see that she has a sense of humor. Observe her use of details and dialogue to create a picture for us. This student attended Villanova University near Philadelphia.*

Hello #1 Granddaughter

The familiar litany of my grandparents' house lets us know we have arrived at the right place.

"Hi kids come on in! Oh goodness. Hurry. It's freezing outside and you don't have a hat on," my grandmother says to us. To my grandfather she says, "Ed! What are you doing? You're making a mess in my kitchen. If you think I'm cleaning that up, you're crazy."

"Oh, Ellen, it's the secret step in all my recipes. Hee, hee, hee," says my grandfather. And then, "Come here kids, I think Grandpa has got some candy in his pocket. Shh…"

I walk by the neat and tidy living room—pillows fluffed (twice), fresh vacuum streaks on the fluffy maroon carpet, and the cabinet of precious polished Chinese figurines. One rule to keep in mind at Grandma's house, never touch, go near, jump near, or play near the cabinet. I make my way to the kitchen, past the smoky atmosphere of all the wonderful smells that make up Grandpa's cooking. The scents and spices of Asian cuisine waft toward my nose. My dad always says that the best Chinese Restaurant is no other than "Ed's Kitchen."

I skip down to the basement where I find the same memorable toys that have miraculously lasted through all 12 grandchildren. I smile to think that I played with these when I was a baby, and how out-of-date they look now. Next to the toy chest is the "Singer" sewing machine, an ancient peculiar invention, from my point of view. But to my grandma it was a way to provide clothing for her family. My mother has told me many stories about how Grandma made her five daughters matching Sunday dresses, or how together they made my mother's prom gown, or how the sheets on the bed upstairs were put together from pieces of material used differently decades ago.

There were many nights that I remember spending in one of those beds, always to wake up early and be the first to greet Grandpa in the morning while he fixed breakfast and while I pointed out where he had cut himself shaving, or if he missed a belt loop. He'd laugh and shrug it off. The Chan family says Grandpa is the happiest man in the world; the house could be on fire and he would be standing there, grin on his face, hands clasped in front of him, enjoying the wonderful heat. On those sleep-over mornings Grandma would be the next to come into the kitchen, and every day Grandpa would say,

"Hey, Ellen, would you like some melon?" And we'd laugh and wait for the roll of her eyes and the tug of a hidden smile.

My grandpa is one of my most favorite people in the world. He is a wise man, a former teacher and mentor, with the most patience and happiness that I have ever seen. We would sit in the basement and he would watch any sports game that was on, even with his minimal knowledge of athletics.

"That Happy Johnson is quite a dribbler...," he would say.

"Um, Grandpa, I think it's *Magic* Johnson." I'd sit there and hold his hand. I wasn't exactly a fan of ESPN but sitting next to Grandpa is something that no one would ever pass up. We could sit for hours and he would talk about anything that came to mind, history lessons, family stories, or things about me that he somehow remembered.

Every time I walked through the door he would take his great big hands and hold my face, kiss me on the forehead and say,

"Hello #1 Granddaughter." Of course he's not one to play favorites, but I am the oldest grandchild and he reminds me that it's something special and something to keep in mind as I influence my younger cousins.

My Grandma is very funny; she has such spunk and spice in her personality for such a small, reserved woman. She's not afraid to speak her mind. She can jump in on a conversation and make fun of her five sons-in-law as if she were one of the men. I admire her self-confidence and audacity. As a somewhat passive person, myself, I look up to my grandma—a tiny elderly Chinese women who one would assume was quiet and conservative. Little does one know she is full of life and full of zest and passion.

There is so much that I realize I've learned from my grandparents as I think about it, now, as a young adult. If I can have just a quarter of my grandpa's patience with my family and half of his enthusiasm for life then I will be satisfied. If I can develop into the woman my grandmother is then I will have her confidence and boldness. As a woman in this tricky world I hope I succeed and make it as well as she does. My grandparents are two completely opposite people. My grandpa is a go-with-the-flow kind of guy; my grandma knows what she wants and could defend herself in the middle of a crowded battlefield. They bicker and disagree, but everyone knows it's nothing serious. Knowing that two different people can be so in love and produce such a beautiful family gives me confidence that their relationship can be duplicated, hopefully in my own life. If I am lucky enough in this manner, then I know I will have their wonderful influence to thank.

Essay 7

The essay is about physical hardship and is the story of a woman who was forced to miss a month of school, right when it was time to bear down and prepare for AP tests. In this essay we not only see her persistence, but her sense of humor and her ability to read others when she goes to see her teacher. None of this is "said"—instead it is revealed in and through the story. And the story is a good one; it held my interest. Despite the fact that her SATs were not as high as she had hoped, the woman who wrote this essay was accepted at all of the colleges to which she applied. Maybe it was her essay! She attended the University of Southern California.

I studied for my AP U.S. History exam by sleeping 20 hours a day, watching television when I did wake up, and fasting for three weeks. I had been staying at Massachusetts General Hospital for a month instead of going to school every day. Certainly my doctors didn't understand that having major pancreatic surgery the second semester of my junior year would make it impossible to catch up in school once I got back, never mind take the SAT, and I figured that my chances of ace-ing the AP U.S. History exam were slim, if not impossible. Fortunately, I slept enough to not think about the academic challenges that lay ahead.

However, I didn't waste all my time while I was in the hospital. I actually learned a lot, just not that much about U.S. History. For example, night nurses have higher salaries than day nurses. If you watch CNN in the afternoon for four hours straight, the news footage will repeat itself at least six times. And looking toward the future, I even prepared myself for college by learning "roommate etiquette."

After a month in the hospital, my surgeon gave my mom the discharge papers, and I was on my way, back to my normal life. I was thankful to be free of the IVs, the blood tests, and the 4 a.m. vital signs checks, but all I could think about on the three hour drive back home to

Connecticut was: How am I going to be ready for the AP U.S. History exam?

When I met privately with my history teacher, I was anything but reassured.

"Gina, you've missed a month of classes, several chapter tests, and you need to make up about 150 pages of reading in your textbook. Not only do you have to catch up but you also need to prepare for the AP exam, and you only have two weeks to do it," he exclaimed.

"What should I do?" I asked. I was aware that my teacher had provided a perfect summary of my dire situation, but I was hoping for some direction as to how I should solve all of the problems.

"Well, you're going to have to take the test. I mean, it's too late now, you signed up! It's too bad the registration deadline was before this whole incident happened. Otherwise, I would have told you not to take the test."

But I didn't want to get out of the test, and my teacher's words affronted me. I, as they say in DBQs, questioned the validity of his statement. Granted, I had spent the past month in the hospital, and I couldn't name any of the alphabet agencies of the New Deal. But, I had been taking this course for eight months, and I wasn't going to let all of my effort go to waste.

"Okay, then I'll take it. So what if I only get a 3? I have nothing to lose."

"You have nothing to lose. If you get a 3, then I'm a bad teacher. But if you get a 5, then I'm a worthless teacher, because you would have learned it all on your own."

"How about a 4? It's a compromise." I joked, hoping to ease my anxiety as I began to leave the classroom. He simply shrugged, and I walked down the hallway wondering how I should best prepare in the limited time I was given.

So I took the test.

At midnight on July 1, I called the AP hotline to get my score. I remember my fingers shaking as I dialed in my registration number. Finally a robot-like voice answered. "Your score is ..."

I probably stopped breathing during the long pause that followed the automated message...

"5."

Essay 8

The student who wrote the following story took on an extra-curricular commitment that was particularly demanding in terms of time and day of the week. Every Saturday he hosted an eight-year-old, who had a disorganized family situation, for an afternoon activity. The student's devotion to this commitment was tireless. On the few Saturdays when he absolutely could not be available, he did not cancel the Saturday date, but got one of his friends to fill in for him. The loyalty that the young eight-year-old felt for the student is clear in this essay, not because the student tells us so, but through the incidents and details in the story that he chooses to relate. The student clearly shows us that when he takes on a responsibility or makes a friend, he is "there" for that friend. The student who wrote this essay attended Middlebury College.

Smiling Through a Face Full of Snow

Dale is eight years old and his favorite activity at my house is going on our very large swing. It's the simple things he appreciates most, the things he never gets a chance to do, such as playing with my dogs, my ancient toy cars, or a basketball. Most of all, it's the attention he craves, the attention kids don't get when their mom is constantly working, their dad is across the country, and they are continuously pushed aside by five siblings. Taking Dale out of his hectic life, if only for a couple of hours each Saturday, and letting him be the center of attention in our close relationship is something he loves and cherishes.

It has been six months since I received the letter from the program that eventually led me to Dale. I took up the role of being his "big friend" within a couple weeks of the arrival of that letter. Since then, Dale and I have seen each other almost every week, and have grown very close. On this particular Saturday, a deep layer of snow covers every bit of my surroundings, the intense sun trying to fight it all off with its piercing rays. I can tell Dale loves this kind of weather by the look on his face as he comes running out of his dilapidated home. He eagerly jumps into the car, and we are off.

I've learned after all my time with Dale that scheduled events and activities aren't what are best for him. He has the most fun relaxing at my house, where everything we do is spur of the moment, whatever he feels like doing on any given Saturday. Today, as soon as we pull into my driveway, Dale eagerly jumps out of his seat into a foot of snow, which covers his worn through jeans but doesn't wipe the smile off his face. He has spotted the sledding trail that my family has made in our front yard, which ends in a large, ice-covered jump. I know exactly what we will be doing for the rest of our time together. I quickly run to get the snow tubes while he follows one step behind.

Sprinting with his snow tube in hand, and looking back at me every few steps to make sure I'm following, Dale approaches the mound where the trail begins. As I watch him step up onto the mound, still smiling, I think about how many opportunities in his life he has had to be able to let go like this, how many times he's been able to slide down an icy snow trail with no worries at all. Based on what I know about Dale's life, there haven't been many, and it gives me great pleasure to be giving him that rare opportunity. It's a feeling I get every week as we enjoy the things I've been able to enjoy my whole life, never realizing or maybe never accepting that there were kids like Dale out there who don't have the same privileges that I so often take advantage of. He lets out a yell of excitement as he slides down the packed snow, gaining speed and approaching that final jump. Finally, he hits it, and soars through the air with immense joy, eventually landing softly on the snow.

The tube stops abruptly as the base of a large oak tree, and he rolls off it, submerging into the light snow. Within a second, however, he is back on his feet, and I can still see that satisfying smile and hear his laughter through a face full of snow. "That was awesome!" he yells, but he didn't have to say it, I knew exactly how he felt. Within a minute he is back up on the mound and I join him this time. We both fly off the mound with ease and soar down the hill together.

After a couple of hours of going up and down the trail, no ride less satisfying than the last for Dale, it's time to head back to his house. We grab a cup of hot chocolate with extra marshmallows and we're on our way. Dale is still riding his emotional high, and about five minutes into the drive back, he exclaims, "This is the best afternoon we've ever had together." And then, he asks me, "Do you think I'm a good kid Nick?" It was as if he was making sure we could have more times like this afternoon, and we would. I'd like to think that in our time together, I can always offer him a simple sledding trail. "Of course," I said.

Essay 9

Sometimes, in a college essay, it is necessary to explain something from the student's application materials which the student does not particularly want to draw attention to, but is so obvious it has to be explained. An example might be a report card with low grades, accompanied by standardized test scores that indicate a high potential for learning. Essay 9 was written by a young man who had very strong SAT scores, but who was so smart he had gotten through school without learning how to study. He wrote this essay to explain some low marks from 9th and 10th grade. Because his writing ability is obvious in this story and because his intended major was journalism/ English, this essay proved to be both an explanation and a demonstration of his skill in controlling voice. The voice he uses might be considered somewhat arrogant, but its humor and confidence are unmistakable. The student was accepted at New York University in New York City.

By the time I got to high school, I was accustomed to coasting. In fact, I reveled in it. Who could tell me to work? I was one of the 50 smartest kids in America, as chosen by Fox TV (I appeared on a television show, "Challenge of the Child Geniuses," which aired in 2002 and was hosted by Dick Clark. Smart kids from national

73

schools were recruited to compete[1]), and I was going to be as lazy as my intelligence allowed me to be. It wasn't just my choice. By God, it was my birthright.

Some people would consider the 78 in Honors Bio glaring at me from my second-semester freshman report card with furious eyes a wake-up call. Then, when my sophomore year schedule arrived with no honors courses on it at all, the blow to my excessive confidence was complete. My brain realized that I couldn't coast anymore. Unfortunately, my soul still needed some convincing.
These two disparate body parts soon became engaged in a struggle against one another for control of my free time. My brain would intone, "No matter how smart you are you still have to study," while my soul would implore me to view the Bluth family's recent misadventures and read about Billy Pilgrim becoming unstuck in time. I was engrossed in Vonnegut, Roth, Maugham (*The Razor's Edge* would become my favorite book), Greene, and Joyce, so engrossed I had no time to listen to the cautionary warnings my brain was insistently delivering to me. Slowly, though, my brain began to convince my soul that studying might actually be a decent idea. Also, that homework thing? It might help my grades if I at least attempted to do it every night. This was the message my brain was transmitting to my soul, and eventually it got through.

But even if realizing you suffer from excessive confidence is half the battle, you still have to learn to correct the ingrained laziness. When you've never really

---

[1] At the time of its airing, this show was described by a salon.com reviewer as putting "serious geekdom on display." I can't say I disagree with this assessment.

studied before, it's almost impossible to simply pick up a history textbook and, three hours later, be prepared for a test on the fall of the Roman Empire. I tried everything, but every traditionally successful technique was, frankly, horrifically ineffective.

It turned out that my addiction to sloth couldn't be solved on my own. I needed an intervention, and it came in the shape of my tutor. She taught me the one thing that altered my perspective on studying, and this simple realization changed everything. I was an auditory learner. When I understood this, everything made sense. This was why my flashcards had absolutely no effect; this was why I could never just study out of a textbook. I needed to hear instead of see.

Suddenly, my productivity expanded vastly. It was no problem for me to study the American Revolution, as long as I was reading to myself out of the textbook. Sure, it garnered a few awkward looks in the library, but it was worth it. And soon I learned that I didn't necessarily have to hear it out loud, as long as I read it to myself in my head. My grades improved dramatically. My average jumped several points, and I never got another C after that initial fall from grace. In fact, my old nemesis, science, even became easy. After my lackluster showing in Biology and a slightly better but still disappointing performance in Chemistry, I excelled in Physics.

I learned more than just study skills from this whole experience, though. I learned that in life, the best way usually isn't the easiest way. More often than not, it's the one with the rattlesnakes and the wooly mammoths. I had been content to wander around the scenic route, not realizing that at the end of the more treacherous path were endless rewards. I was so embroiled in how easy my life was that I neglected to realize that I was wasting long-term adventure for temporary escape. I won't make that mistake again—from now on, I'm going to brave the harder trail, because the easy way out isn't that satisfying, is it?

Essay 10

The intimate and authentic voice of this story teller is obvious. And her use of details is great. From the first sentence, you feel you are in the car with her, seeing the things she sees, the pink plastic bowl, the single yellow flip-flop. During the course of the story, two stories, really, we share in her realizations about life—the one in the beginning when she thinks she has it figured out, and the second one when she admits to knowing she doesn't have it figured out. Look for the sentence that keeps us reading, that makes us want to go on; it occurs fairly early, but not at the beginning. She says, "Three years ago I would have told you that this was the moment that changed my life… But…" So this is a kind of a mid-story hook. This student was accepted through early decision to Middlebury College in Vermont.

It's Definitely Not a Saving People Thing

It's sticky and humid, but that's to be expected. This is the Philippines after all. The car's AC is on full blast, but sweat still clings to my back. Seat belts are optional and strongly discouraged. The street is wide, lined by palm trees. Beyond the tropical fauna, houses are visible in the Spanish style: cool tile roofs and inner courtyards, fountains and fish ponds.

We pass beyond the walls surrounding the wealthy enclave into Manila. Skyscrapers abound. Traffic is, as usual, horrendous. In Manila, driving is a creative art

76

and everyone has his own style. Colorful jeep-neys, public buses, pass in their vibrant grafittied glory. The car jolts to a stop at a light, and we're grateful the windows are up. Children swarm the gridlocked vehicles, hawking food of questionable origin. They are not in school, though public school is in session.

Then, Glorietta Mall: Abercrombie, Guess, Ralph Lauren, Gap, Chanel, myriad boutiques. This mall could easily be found near any major American city. And surrounding one side of the mall: shantytowns--tin shacks and barefoot children, a pink plastic bowl left in the dust, in one doorway, a single yellow flip flop.

Three years ago I would have told you that this was the moment that changed my life: becoming fully aware of the poverty that is all too common in developing nations focused my otherwise vague desire to "become a writer." I wouldn't be just any writer; I'd be a writer with a purpose. Armed with my trusty pen I would singlehandedly enlighten the world about the plight of the impoverished. I'd be a journalist. And, oh yes, I'd save the world. But then, my sophomore year I went on a trip to help build a school in Nicaragua and everything changed.

The village was built on a mountain. The houses, huts really, were built topsy turvy, pell mell, falling one over the other on the cliff edge. Everything was green and growing and overgrown. The huts stuck out like drab brown blots in a sea of verdant fertility.

Days were busy. The men went into the fields to tend the corn or coffee crops, my host mother cooked and cleaned, and so far as I could tell my nine year old host sister roamed the village.

But mornings were my favorite. We emerged from our hammocks and mosquito netting at 5:00 A.M. The sun was not fully risen; fog rolled in waves over the mountains, climbed up mud house walls, and cast rope-like tendrils at people's feet. My host mother, Petronilla, would already have been in the kitchen hut for an hour, and through chinks in the plank walls came the familiar sound of pad, pad, pad as she cooked our meal: beans, rice, and tortillas. We held hot coffee in our dirty, unshowered hands and clustered outside at the back of the house. This miraculously flat patch of ground was the scene of every village gathering, every party, and some of the most interesting conversations I had while in Nicaragua.

Perhaps I loved the mornings most for those calm moments. Village life was slow compared to the hectic lifestyle back home. Don't get me wrong; I love being busy. Still, there's something to be said for taking the time to just *be*.

The villagers are experts at "being." They have an entire lifetime in rural Nicaragua to hone their skills. Nearly everyone is related by blood or marriage. Relationships aren't a luxury; they're essential.

It's easy to equate poverty with misery. I know I did. Ever since the Philippines my calling seemed clear. Poverty was bad. I'd help end poverty. Except...poverty is a lot more complex than a few assumptions based on some shocked glances out a car window. It's complicated. It's difficult. And yet, despite the Nicaraguan children's stomachs, bloated by malnutrition, their lives are lives of contentment. The villagers are some of the happiest people I've met.

So tackling poverty is definitely not a saving people thing. Help, yes. Save, no. Learn, definitely.

Essay 11

The student who wrote the story below was a superior athlete. He got drafted to his high school's varsity soccer team when its regular goalie, a few days before the season began, was hurt and could not return for the season. Yet, more than highlighting his athletic ability, the writer of this essay wanted to let the admissions committees know about his regard for people and his spiritual faith. As it turned out, the student became a player on his college's Ultimate Frisbee Team and played for them when they went to the national finals for this sport. This essay lets you see not only the athletic ability of this student and his spiritual faith, but his kind spirit toward his fellow human beings. Be sure to observe the author's use of short, declarative sentences to simulate the action in the first section. The essay is very long, it is true. What part would you recommend that he eliminate? This student attended the University of Wisconsin in Madison.

Out of Bounds

Rain is blinding us, and our feet keep slipping on the wet, muddy ground. But still we run on, me and John, John and me, sprinting faster and faster. I am offense, he is defense. We both strain our heads back to see the disc go flying over our heads and follow it on its quest to make one of us, and break the other. We run on, stride for stride. My one thought is catching it, and his is making sure that I don't. It's the ultimate battle of wills, who wants it more. We are best friends, but this is war. We know that after this play is over we'll be laughing and patting each other on the back, but it's not over yet.

79

We finally catch up with it, our legs burning with the pain that comes from sprinting that far, and we dive. I get the upper hand, and snatch it right out of the air, out of his grasp, and right before it meets with gravity. The day is mine; I am on top of the world.

This is why Frisbee holds a special place in my heart, and always will. It's two teams, battling each other and the white piece of plastic, searching for the glory that only this sport can bring. There are boundaries, but not as most think of them. The boundaries are the woods, or where the field ends, and the road starts. But if the play is good enough, and someone's effort and desire overcomes the threat of trees or cars, we let them play on. It's almost like a leap of faith. The leaper's hopes being, of course, that 1) he doesn't get hurt by whatever he's jumping into and 2) that, no matter what obstacle may lie in his way that he will catch the disc.

In the game I am always the one that goes diving after the Frisbee with reckless abandon, not caring what obstacles may lie beneath me: be they rocks, thorns or trees. Sometimes I make the play, and sometimes I don't, but without risking defeat you will never be victorious. Above all you must make yourself vulnerable. If you truly want to make the catch, that must be the only thing in your mind; you can't be afraid of failure, you have to believe that in the end it will all work out.

When I stop to think, I realize that relationships are also a leap, or leaps of faith. In order to form a meaningful relationship, whether with a female or male, you really must make yourself vulnerable and let them into your very "self." Sometimes, just as in Frisbee, you'll make the connection, and that person may, in the end be someone you marry, or ask to be your best man, or grow old with. But other times, you'll get hurt. You'll dive into the relationship with the hope of a great connection, or a true friend, but fall hard into the rocks and thorns below. But you have to make the leap. You really never know. Someone who you never thought that you could have a meaningful relationship with could turn out to be the best friend that you ever had, and could be with you for the rest of your life, just as a catch you never thought you'd make, but went for anyway, could be a play talked about among your peers long after the game is through.

Relationships with other people, however, aren't the most important or most difficult leap that I have had to go for. My hardest leap, with the most pitfalls below, is the leap that I have made, and will continue to make towards the world of faith. It's a leap that doesn't just decide a nice catch or even a great friend, but is really a matter of life or death. In Paul's letter to the Hebrews he writes that "Faith is being sure of what we hope for and certain of what we do not see." In many ways this connects directly to playing Frisbee. God calls us to go diving after him with all that we are, despite what people might say, or how difficult it is. The only promise that He makes to us is that if we have faith in Him we'll be saved from the disaster and that His reward will even be better than the praise that comes from risking life and limb playing Frisbee. A wise man once said that "When you come to the edge of all the light you have, and must take a step into the darkness of the unknown, believe that one of two things will happen to you; either there will be something firm to stand on or you will be taught how to fly."

But, you have to believe in everything you do. When if running after a Frisbee sailing uncontrollably into the woods, you are concerned about getting hurt, you won't be able to make the play. It's the same with faith. You

81

have to dive for God, and realize that everything is possible with Him. In the end the option is clear. You can either stand on the edge of the field and the woods, watching as your opportunity for a great catch, a true friend or the love of God passes you by, or you can fling yourself fearlessly into the forest with your eye fixed on your goal. As for me, I am in the woods, amidst the terrors and the fears that are present here. But I am not worried. Not because I have a firm place to stand, but because with the grace of God I can soar above the dangers without fear that He'll ever let me go.

Essay 12

Listen to the voice that tells this story. I think you will agree that the student who wrote this story has succeeded in finding his true voice. Besides being honest, he is also witty, sarcastic, and a master of understatement. And just as important are the details he uses to tell us about the boys in his troop and the new activities he fines to engage and teach them. His acuity and ability to make adjustments, as well as his maturity and creative problem solving ability are obvious in these details. Finally the pace of the essay is quick and upbeat—it is quick, that is, until we get to the last paragraph. The last paragraph, it seems to me, slows the piece down; in fact, much of it is unnecessary. This student, like others who complete an essay, thinks that he is not really done until he restates its purpose. That is because students fall back into the five-paragraph-essay mentality. In this case, we already know the student worked harder than he wanted to, yet, grew to be an effective leader; he has shown us this. So I would eliminate his last three sentences in the final paragraph, and keep the first two. That he would have wanted to be in his own troop as a scout and that the troop had had the best year in recent memory are marks of his effective leadership, without actually restating this. I think he should

82

*have been done when he got to this point. This student attended
the University of Maryland in College Park, Maryland.*

Before I had even finished tying the first knot, Ryan was
standing up, demanding that the rope be passed around.
There was no doubt in my mind that he did not actually
want to practice tying anything but rather distract
himself by maliciously flicking his eleven year old
friends. I was the newly appointed Senior Patrol Leader,
standing in front of twenty out-of-control young Boy
Scouts, who by the end of their day could not have sat
still to save their own lives. They were punching each
other's shoulders, kicking each other's legs, and asking
questions relevant to something only in their
imaginations. It was great to be in charge.

I had started off sitting right where they were when I
joined the Boy Scouts as a fifth grader so I understood
all about the game of not letting the authority "be" in
authority. In fact, I immediately recognized these tactics
from many of my high school classes where I had been
adept at accomplishing the same goal. Now, I had come
a long way from sitting on the floor, fidgeting with my
neighbor, and I was in charge of the entire troop. From
the start, I can't say I was very excited. The amount of
work and patience required had greatly surpassed my
expectations.

It was 8:30 pm on Monday night. After an hour of
relentless mocking and horseplay we had accomplished
nothing. Everyone, including me, wanted to go home.
The only way to save this dismal situation was to
introduce something that was more fun than goofing off.
I told everyone to stand up and get into three lines.
Those half-listening jumped at the invite to stand, and
those not listening rose, following the others, so as to

not indicate they were, in fact, not listening at all. Everyone was up and moving. I announced we were going to do a relay race. The first person would run to the end of the room, tie a certain knot with a piece of rope on the floor, and run back to tag the next player. This exercise confirmed that no one had taken away any knowledge from my hour-long demonstration. However, it was promising in that the boys had done what I asked and had fun while doing it. Lying on the floor exhausted at the end of the night, dreading the task of putting the tangles of rope back into their bags, I realized I had to incorporate something more hands-on in future lessons.

So, by the end of the year typical lectures had long been forgotten. Competitions dominated as a mode of teaching and group bragging rights became the motive to participate. Something as simple as setting up a tent soon became how quickly could a group set one up in the dark. It was a contest, but also pounded home important and practical skills. Instead of reading about wilderness survival, we made our own shelters in the parking lot and compared. Cooking lessons over camp-stoves became episodes of *Iron Chef*. Water safety lessons became one partner in the pool as the victim while the other swam out to rescue the first, hoping to be named *Baywatch*'s next guest star. Another notable contest was who can save the victim best, whether he was a victim of anything from lightning strike to heart-attack. The fireman's carry became a race for the "gold," and making a simple splint with a bandana wasn't enough—mock victims soon passed for ancient mummies, as casts and slings decorated every bone on their bodies.

Needless to say, our typical monthly camping trips were not enough to hold the boys' interests. High adventure escapes were soon the norm, as we conquered rapids, rock-walls, ocean waves, and blizzards. Rafting, canoeing, kayaking, how to live on an island, and hiking through snowstorms soon became first-hand knowledge to all the boys. None of this was taught through lecture, none of it could have been. Everything the boys learned they discovered through "in-the-field" experiences.

At the end of the year as I evaluated my effectiveness as a leader and the growth of the troop, I realized I wished I could have been a boy in the troop while I was in charge. This had been the best year in the troop since I could remember. I also realized I had grown tremendously as a leader. However, leading the troop was very difficult and much more work than I ever imagined, but if you want a better experience someone has to step up.

Essay 13

The following story is one of the best essays I have read that answers the questions: Why do you want to study on our campus? What things do you see yourself doing on our campus? Remember what I said at the outset of this book—this is not the kind of question usually asked in the personal essay. However, I thought you might like to see an answer to a supplemental question as the student who wrote this has such an authentic voice that the essay sparkles. She answers the questions so eloquently and with such heartfelt sincerity that we are with her every step of the way as she plunges into her inspired quest of discovery. This student is attending Princeton University in Princeton, New Jersey, although this essay was written for a different university's application.

Applicants: Please relate your interest in studying at our university to your goals. How do these thoughts relate to your chosen course of study?

No Title

This essay topic makes me think of a poem I read recently by Pablo Neruda. The last two lines read, "I wheeled with the stars, my heart broke loose on the wind."[2] The rush of emotions the author is feeling in those last two lines comes from a moment of instant clarification, in which he is told exactly what to do with his life. The subject of the poem is especially meaningful to me—here I am trying to decide the rest of my life, as I fill out college applications which are asking me about plans for my future, and Neruda is just handed his destiny. As a reader, I too feel the exhilaration he must have experienced at finding where he belonged. While I might not know exactly where I belong just yet, I know where I am heading; I know that my own heart breaks loose on the wind whenever I learn something new.

Learning new things inspires me. I live for tackling challenges, absorbing and synthesizing knowledge, and unveiling hidden truths. I have never met a subject I didn't like – how can you dislike some new puzzle that's just waiting to be pieced together? Even while struggling in Honors Physics, the hardest class I have ever taken, I still got chills of excitement whenever I found the concept or equation that would unlock the problem's mystery. That moment when everything just "clicks" is completely rewarding.

As I said, learning new things inspires me–and there are so many new things that, perhaps, this is why I have not yet been able to pinpoint a particular academic passion. However, my experience working at Yale University's Child Study Center did ignite a passion for a particular

---

[2] From "Poetry" by Pablo Neruda

subject–the study of human behavior and the brain (neuropsychology). The connection between the biological functions, physical structures, and psychological consequences of the brain fascinates me. The humanizing element of this field also commands my attention–studying something that actually affects people's everyday lives makes it that much more worthwhile. I can see myself at Georgetown learning more about this field and then further exploring what I've learned by conducting research.

I can see myself sprinting across the campus after a European history class to finish up some research in the lab, then later that night meeting up with friends for coffee to discuss both the newest episode of "Grey's Anatomy" and which presidential candidate's health care plan makes the most sense. I can see myself meeting the sunrise for our morning run along the river, reciting different mathematic formulas with each step.

I sometimes wish I could just be handed a destiny like Neruda, but after further consideration, I realize that determining my own future is a journey I can't wait to take. I don't know what my chosen course of study is–I know that I love research, in all of its many forms. I also know that I have the enthusiasm, and perseverance, and resourcefulness, and leadership skills to excel. So let the future begin.

Reminder

Just a quick reminder: the last essay, #13, which you have just read is not an example of the personal essay that we have been discussing throughout this book. Although it certainly contains many personal ideas, this is an essay which answers a question often asked by colleges on their supplement to the common application—they say something to the effect of: why is our college a good match for you and what do you intend to study here? Since you know that this type of question will be forth coming in the supplemental part of the common application, it is in your best interest to avoid this kind of answer in the personal statement section of the commonapp. Instead use the personal statement section to tell your story and to foster and promote a connection with the reader so that you will distinguish yourself and be remembered.

Chapter 5

PARTING WORDS

A student who read an early manuscript for this book said she felt there was something missing at the end of the book. She said, "I would also add something to conclude the book—like final words to the reader instead of just ending with the last essay."

I think I know what she meant. We have established a kind of relationship—you and I. I have been pulling for you and encouraging you in this search for yourself and in finding your story and your voice. Also I have invited you to celebrate who you are, free from the conventional five-paragraph high school essay. Additionally, I have been encouraging you to think about me as a possible imaginary coach for your brain storming, and as a possible audience for your soon to be completed essay.

I know what sometimes happens when a student is freed to say and think and be his or her real self because sometimes parents tell me stories about their students, who have been struggling all summer, trying to write a personal college admissions essay. After the student comes to me to hear about the writing process that I have described to you in this book, he or she goes home and begins writing up a storm. One mom said that when her daughter got home, the daughter ate dinner and then stayed up all night writing. When she came to see me the next week she had six extraordinary essays—six essays to choose among. Most students come back with somewhat less writing, but interestingly, there are always wonderful sentences with true glimpses of the real student. Touching stories and memorable moments have been remembered and written down. The real student, like the real Huck Finn, shows up with the beginnings of a "wow" essay.

So my wish for you is that you, too, will feel inspired and liberated by the method described in this book and that you will absolutely find your narrative voice and capture your personal story. I know that if your essay is "so me," as my student Mark would say, you will connect with your college admissions counselor. Also should you want to share with me, I would be pleased to receive a copy of your essay.

I wish you the sense of freedom that comes with the celebration of your true self.

Appendices

Appendix A—Who Are You?

Look at the following characteristics to see which of them you think might apply to you. Circle the ones you think might describe you. Then go back and think to yourself, "Okay, if I had to tell a story that demonstrates how this characteristic applies to me, what would it be?" This is when you need to remember the advice your English teacher has been giving you all these years, "*Show, don't tell.*" If you think that you are collaborative, tell the story of the time, for instance, that you and a friend worked to solve a difficulty between two other friends. If you think you are a positive person, tell about an incident that might have gotten someone else down, but which you overcame by using your positive approach. Then actually write a page on each of the four or five best stories you have to tell. If one of these is a standout, you have the beginning of an essay. If nothing seems to sound good, try using the process described in Appendix B.

Accepting	Conscientious	Friendly
Aggressive	Cooperative	Fun-loving
Altruistic	Courageous	Genuine
Analytical	Creative	Go with the flow
Artistic	Curious	Grounded
Athletic	Dedicated	Happy
Calm	Determined	Helpful
Camp-able	Diligent	Homebody
Candid	Distant	Honorable
Capable	Dramatic	Hopeful
Careful	Easy-going	Humorous
Casual	Energetic	Imaginative
Cheerful	Enthusiastic	Impulsive
Compassionate	Entrepreneurial	Independent
Competitive	Extroverted	Informal
Concerned	Faithful	Informed

Confident	Focused	Initiator
Conformist	Formal	Insightful
Intellectual	Passive	Serious
Intense	Patient	Shy
Introverted	Perceptive	Sincere
Involved	Placid	Smooth
Kind	Planner	Sociable
Leader	Poised	Sophisticated
Level-headed	Political	Supportive
Loyal	Principled	Tactful
Mature	Procrastinator	Talkative
Multi-tasker	Proud	Thoughtful
Open	Rabble-rouser	Tolerant
Optimist	Receptive	Unique
Organized	Reflective	Upbeat
Original	Relaxed	Warm
Outdoorsy	Resilient	Witty
Outgoing	Self-confident	
Passionate	Sensitive	

Appendix B—What Has Happened to You?
Be sure you explain <u>why</u> or <u>how</u> for each of the answers you give below.

1. How do you compare to your peers? Do any activities or thoughts distinguish you from others your age? Explain.

2, Are you a fencer, a surfer, a pastry chef, a chess player, a harpist? Or what exceptional talent do you have in music, art, drama, athletics or another area? What do you know, and possibly take for granted, that others might not even suspect that you know? What might you tell them that you think they should know from what you have learned or experienced?

3. How do your parents and/or friends describe you? What do they like about you? Do you agree with them?

4. Describe the biggest challenge or hardship you have faced? How have you come through it and what, if anything, did you learn about yourself?

5. Do you have any heroes? What makes them heroic?

6. What is your favorite quote? Why and how has it helped you?

7. What activity, subject, or country do you wish you knew more about?

8. What lessons have you learned? How?

9. Who has influenced you in your life? What qualities do you admire in this person?

10. What do you need to be happy?

11. What is your philosophy of life?

12. How have you grown through the course of high school?

13. If you were given the time and resources to develop one particular skill, talent or area of expertise, what would it be?

14. What is the extra-curricular or summer activity you most enjoy? Explain.

15. Tell us something we might not have learned from the rest of your application.

16. How have you contributed to your community either at school or outside of school?

17. What fears have you had? How have you handled them? What is the outcome?

18. What is the best advice you had ever received? How has it influenced your life?

19. Describe the personal experience that has given you the greatest satisfaction.

20. A "keeper" is a movie or book that can be watched or read over and over; it has lasting value. It might be one of the things you would take to a desert island if you knew you were going to be there for six months. Discuss some of your keepers. What do you like about them?

21. What is your favorite place or way to relax? Talk about this.

22. You know what a "do-over" is. It occurs when something interferes with the forward or expected motion of play or an event, and everyone agrees to go back where they were and do the whole thing over. Are there any things in your life that you wish you could do over?

Appendices

Appendix C—Recommended Resources

Web sites: With Good Information on Admissions Essays

Oregon State "Insight Resume"
(http://oregonstate.edu/admissions/publications/insight_resume
_worksheet.pdf)
Read the six thoughtful questions and see if you want to write
on any of these.

University of Virginia
(www.virginia.edu/undergradadmission/writingtheessay)
See the rest of Parke Muth's advice about essays. And read
some sample essays.

Tufts University (www.admissions.tufts.edu)
The Office of Admissions has put a good number of successful
essays—essays which worked for them—under the heading
"Discovering Voice: Essays That Matter."

Connecticut College
(http://www.conncoll.edu/admission/essays.htm)
Read the 10+ admissions essays that Connecticut College has
labeled "Essays that Worked" from the class of 2012.

University of Chicago
(https://collegeadmissions.uchicago.edu/admissions/essays.shtm
l)
This admissions office lists its unique, thought provoking
questions which are new each year. Read this year's and those
of other years.

Books: Books on Writing Techniques or Ideas

Bauld, Harry. *On Writing the College Application Essay*: The
Key to Acceptances in the College of Your Choice. New York:

Barnes and Noble, 1987. Hale, Constance. *Sin and Syntax, How to Craft Wickedly Effective Prose.* New York: Broadway Books, 1999. Look for Hugh Gallagher's College Essay.

Mason, Michael James. *How to Write a Winning College Application Essay.* Roseville: Prima Publishing, 2000.

Zinsser, William. *On Writing Well: An Informal Guide to Writing Nonfiction.* New York: Harper Collins, 1995. Look for the chapter on first lines, e.g., "In the beginning God created heaven and earth…"

Examples of Good Speaking and Writing

Steve Jobs Stanford Graduation Speech—2005
http://news.stanford.edu/news/2005/june15/jobs-061505

"This I Believe"
http://thisibelieve.org/essaywritingtips.html

Appendices

Appendix D—The Author

Jan Rooker

Jan has been an educational consultant for almost 15 years. Prior to this she taught high school English in Ridgewood, NJ and Woodside, CA. She has advised high school students about colleges for more than 20 years, and has guided more than 1,500 students in writing their admissions essays. She graduated from Cornell University (BA), Stanford University (MA), and Columbia University (MA).

In addition to mentoring high school students, aiding students in learning about and selecting colleges, brain storming college admissions essays, and offering essay writing workshops to large and small groups, she works with individual students on essays by telephone and via the Internet. Her Web site is: www.janrooker.com. Her email is: jan@janrooker.com.